HOPE SQUAD

The Successful Suicide Prevention Program for Youth

DR. GREGORY A. HUDNALL

PLAIN SIGHT
PUBLISHING

An imprint of Cedar Fort, Inc.
Springville, Utah

WITHDRAWN

DEDICATED TO MILINDA
my wife and rock
of thirty-seven years

© 2018 Gregory A. Hudnall
All rights reserved.

No part of this book may be reproduced in any form whatsoever, whether by graphic, visual, electronic, film, microfilm, tape recording, or any other means, without prior written permission of the publisher, except in the case of brief passages embodied in critical reviews and articles.

The opinions and views expressed herein belong solely to the author and do not necessarily represent the opinions or views of Cedar Fort, Inc. Permission for the use of sources, graphics, and photos is also solely the responsibility of the author.

ISBN 13: 978-1-4621-2219-6

Published by Plain Sight Publishing, an imprint of Cedar Fort, Inc.
2373 W. 700 S., Springville, UT 84663
Distributed by Cedar Fort, Inc., www.cedarfort.com

LIBRARY OF CONGRESS CATALOGING-IN-PUBLICATION DATA

Names: Hudnall, Greg, 1958- author.
Title: The hope squad : the successful suicide prevention program for
    students / Greg Hudnall.
Description: Springville, Utah : Plain Sight Publishing, An imprint of Cedar
    Fort, Inc., [2018] | Includes bibliographical references and index.
Identifiers: LCCN 2018025035 (print) | LCCN 2018029201 (ebook) | ISBN
    9781462129263 (epub, pdf, mobi) | ISBN 9781462122196 (perfect bound : alk.
    paper)
Subjects: LCSH: Suicide--Prevention.
Classification: LCC HV6546 (ebook) | LCC HV6546 .H85 2018 (print) | DDC
    362.28/70835--dc23
LC record available at https://lccn.loc.gov/2018025035

Cover design by Jeff Harvey
Cover design © 2018 Cedar Fort, Inc.
Edited by Melissa Caldwell and James Gallagher (Castle Walls Editing LLC)
Typeset by Kaitlin Barwick

Printed in the United States of America

10 9 8 7 6 5 4 3 2 1

Printed on acid-free paper

CONTENTS

PART 4: The Hope Squad: Suicide Is Not an Option

FOREWORD

Preventing youth suicide is hard.

If preventing youth suicide were easy, someone would have done it by now. Many have tried to prevent youth suicide, but few have succeeded, and it is probably closer to none.

Perhaps until now. While it is too soon to confirm through scientific study, I believe Dr. Greg Hudnall is on the brink of at least one major solution to youth suicide: Hope Squads.

In full disclosure, Greg is a colleague, friend, and partner in our shared organizational goal of preventing suicide. We do nothing else. Preventing suicide is our only mission.

Let me tell you why I think Hope Squads have a chance to succeed. First, Hope Squads have a substantial history of success with their problem-solving approach to school-based suicide prevention. Too many organizations have one idea followed by a short history in which they burn out and fail. Hope Squads endure.

Second, Hope Squads stand on a rock-solid scientific foundation of tested educational principles, ecological social network theory, and a humane peer-to-peer action model for positive, youth-led change supported by informed adults.

Third—and in my view, this is key—Hope Squad students are already embedded in their schools and have been selected by their peers for having the "right stuff" to help students in distress. Trained observers who can recognize and respond to suicide warning signs (the QPR part), Hope Squad youth become the "eyes and ears" for the school's adult leadership.

Why does this matter?

Because preventing youth suicide is very much about the early detection of suicide risk long before it leads to fatal planning or a suicide attempt.

Every school has youth who, for reasons not their own, are at elevated risk for suicide. Teachers often know who they are and do everything they can to be helpful. But teachers may only have them in class for one hour a day, and the nature of the teacher–student relationship can be difficult to negotiate when a child is entering a crisis.

But trained Hope Squad members become the benevolent surveillance team of the school. They become an intelligence-gathering squad able to collect critical movements in the lives of their peers. They observe emotional displays, watch relationships break up, and hear about fights with parents. They alone can walk up to a student who may be upset or crying or angry and ask, "Say, George, it looks like you're having a rough day. Can we sit over here and talk about it?"

Few adults can do this or have the time to do it. But peers can, and when trained and supported, they make the time to do it.

Greg Hudnall has a vision for Hope Squads. More, he has made his vision a reality. He has felt the pain of leadership in the aftermath of the preventable loss of life of young people. He has poured his heart and soul into creating a world in which youth can be found, comforted, helped, and made to feel whole again.

This is an important book for three reasons:

1. It is accessible to the average reader, even entertaining. Most academic books on youth suicide are unreadable and filled with unintelligible scientific and psychological jargon.
2. It is anchored in both personal experience and published science, and it is fully annotated with source information so you can delve further into the research.
3. The author is a powerful, honest, and complete and artful storyteller. The candor and truth with which he writes is immediately self-evident. You will not think twice about his sincerity or genuineness.

Finally, public health research has shown again and again that when it comes to changing human behavior, stories are more powerful than statistics. Humans have been storytellers since the beginning of time, and Greg Hudnall ranks among the very best in reaching into our hearts with truth, humor, and, yes, even painful facts that are bound to hurt but that might, just might, help us all save lives.

PAUL QUINNETT, PhD, President and CEO
The QPR Institute, Inc.
Clinical Assistant Professor
University of Washington School of Medicine

ACKNOWLEDGMENTS

I am not a writer; I am a storyteller.

When I was a high school principal, my school had a closed campus. Students were not allowed to leave until school was over and visitors were not allowed on campus. One early spring day, we had a group of beautiful senior girls who were enjoying the spring sun out on the steps of the school.

As people drove by, the girls would flirt and enjoy the attention. A group of construction workers were impressed with these young ladies and stopped by to visit. I happened to be on lunch duty and saw the construction workers get out of their truck. As I walked out of the school, I noticed there were three of them, and they were all suntanned and as huge as trees.

Though I am not very big, others do not intimidate me, so I walked up to them and politely asked them to leave. The biggest, meanest-looking one stepped up to me and said, "Who do you think you are?" Looking at his belt buckle, because he was twice my size, I politely replied that I was the principal and that this was a closed campus and they needed to leave. Of course, they just laughed.

By this time, the students were getting nervous. Unknown to me, one of the girls went back into the school and grabbed a few of the senior boys. Behind my back, a group of my biggest former football players stood at the door and threatened the construction workers with sign language that silently told them to leave. Not seeing or being aware of the students at the door, I again asked the men to leave. This time they apologized and went to their truck.

The senior boys had disappeared by the time I turned around. Thinking I had forced the men to leave, I bragged to the girls, "I guess I showed them." I did not learn until later that day that it was the senior boys who had turned the tide and scared the men away. I was grateful for those amazing young people.

The past twenty-five years in suicide prevention have been the same story and the same experience. Incredible people have opened doors, stood up for the cause, and helped move it forward. Many I have never met, others I met in a fleeting moment, and, gratefully, others I have had the privilege to serve with.

To every one of you, I say thank you.

INTRODUCTION

Success Is Not an Isolated Journey

To the parents and families of suicide victims, I am so sorry for your loss. I have never lost a child or a family member to suicide. There is no blame in the world of suicide. It's a complex, individualized challenge. My goal is not to shame or blame but to share a story that I hope will help prevent suicides.

Not all suicides can be prevented. However, of all deaths, suicide is the one that is most preventable.[1]

When Cedar Fort Publishing called and asked if I were willing to share the Hope Squad story, I was not sure I could. Who would want to hear my story? And did I really want to share it? I have shed so many tears over the years that I was afraid to open up the many wounds I've tried to put out of my mind. These wonderful families that I talk about have each lost a child. The pain for them is real.

This story is a journey over thirty years. I could not share it without including experiences and stories as a son, father, husband, principal, school district employee, friend, and city council member. Suicide prevention became my passion and my life. I do this because I want to save lives.

The cast of characters includes family members, educators, peers, mental health experts, families who have lost children, and, of course, the children who attempted or died by suicide. I'm sure my words cannot even come close to explaining the lifelong pain felt from the loss of a child. My story does not do enough to honor these folks.

A few years ago, I was visiting with the mother and father of a former student who had taken his life by suicide. After a while, the mother looked at me and said through tears, "Dr. Hudnall, I attended your training the other night. I wish I knew then what I know now. Maybe, just maybe, it might have saved my son's life!"

So why did I write this book? I want to start talking about suicide. I want people to understand that of all deaths, suicide is the most preventable. I want everyday people, people like you and me, to understand that they are not the only ones who may struggle with some sort of mental illness, such as depression, anxiety, ADHD, and many others. I want people to be no more ashamed of mental illness than of a broken arm or a sprained ankle.

I also want families of lost loved ones to understand that of the fifty-four youth suicides I have been involved with as either a first responder or a consultant, in almost all cases the kids hid it from their families. They did not want anyone, except maybe a best friend or other confidant, to know that they were struggling.

In most of those cases, the suicide attempt occurred within twenty-four to forty-eight hours of an incident that pushed them to the edge. This might have been a romantic breakup, a disciplinary action, a bully's actions, or a failure at something. And in many of those cases, they had been struggling with some sort of depression or other mental illness.

This story tells how an entire community came together to rally the forces to try to save children's lives. It is not the story of one individual as a hero. It is the story of a community made up of many people. All are equal in recognition.

We all must join this fight together.

Note

1. "Teen Suicide Is Preventable," American Psychological Association, accessed January 19, 2018, http://www.apa.org/research/action/suicide.aspx.

LIFESAVERS

Throughout the book, I have listed "Lifesavers" that are important for us to know and become comfortable with. The purpose of these Lifesavers is to make us more aware of things that will help us aid someone who is struggling. They are the "next step" to helping us better understand and intervene with suicide prevention.

I have included key ingredients for helping us know what we can do to help students, family members, or others who are struggling. Some of the items are lists from mental health experts. While I have added opinions and thoughts from my many experiences, the main content is from the experts.

I have listed them here to serve as a quick reference for readers. Please take the time to review the Lifesavers. The more we understand the protective factors, risk factors, warning signs, and other important topics, the more we are able to prevent suicide.

- Talking about Suicide
- Warning Signs
- Protective Factors and Resiliency
- Risk Factors
- Coping and Problem-Solving Skills
- Common Misconceptions about Suicide
- The Stigma with Mental Illness
- What to Say and What Not to Say
- Crisis Line
- Impulsive Behavior, ADHD, and Suicide
- Train for Suicide Prevention
- Social Media and the Internet
- Dos and Don'ts of Reporting Suicide
- Suicide and Bullying
- Making a Community Impact
- Reduce Access to Lethal Means
- Youth Stressors and Academic Performance Anxiety
- Suicide Risk of LGBTQ Students
- Trauma
- Getting Help for Mental Illnesses and Depression
- Permission Granted

"While it takes an entire village to raise a child, we believe it takes an entire community to save one."

—DR. GREGORY A. HUDNALL

PART 1

The School:
Life Can Be Painful

CHAPTER 1

A Young Principal Aged by Student Suicides

The state of Utah and most of the Northwestern states have been in the top ten states for suicide for over twenty years. Further, seven of those top ten states are in the Intermountain West.[1] In 2017, Utah was ranked fifth for suicide. It is the first leading cause of death for ages ten to twelve in Utah.[2]

One western city that has struggled with high suicide rates is Provo, Utah. Provo is a college town that was settled early on by the Mormons (members of The Church of Jesus Christ of Latter-day Saints). At the beginning of this story, in 1987, the city had about ninety-three thousand residents. About twenty-five thousand were students at Brigham Young University, a private school for The Church of Jesus Christ of Latter-day Saints. Many of the students and much of the city's population are Mormon. Mormons are often characterized as being happy, and this area of Utah is often referred to as "Happy Valley."

If at any time over the past thirty years you were to tell someone that Provo had a problem with kids taking their lives, no one would have believed you.

But my community had been struggling with youth suicide for many years. Unfortunately, we were losing one to two kids a year. We even lost a fourth grader who took his life on campus. The youngest we had attempt suicide was a five-year-old in preschool. While it took its toll, we, the Provo City School District, as an educational system of fourteen thousand students grades K through twelve, became desensitized. We focused on the classroom and felt that the community was responsible for everything else.

Everyone from law enforcement to mental health workers accepted the losses due to suicide. As a community and as a state, we seemed fated to always be in the top ten for suicide across the country. Sometimes I would even hear people brag about it. The press did a nice job of keeping it out of the newspaper.

My story begins when I was the principal of Independence High School. Independence is an alternative high school, or an educational setting for students who struggle in traditional schools. The school consists of about 350 students from two mainstream high schools in the district. For many years, we had been losing kids through the cracks of poor attendance, failing classes, and getting lost in the shuffle of secondary school.

For a while, the community was not supportive of the school. Community members seemed uncomfortable with having so many struggling and nontraditional students. Over time, however, the community became supportive of the school and the kids. It gave us the flexibility to focus on their emotional needs first and their academic abilities second. They were all good kids. Many were just lost and needed individual attention with smaller classrooms.

Interestingly enough, we lost as many students to suicide from the two mainstream high schools and middle schools as we did from Independence High School.

From the beginning, I loved being a principal. I could not wait to get out of bed to be with my kids. Every morning, I would be in front of the school greeting students and waving to parents. My love for the students is what both pushed me to help them and made each suicide hurt more.

One of the first suicides I was involved with was the loss of a young lady who had been struggling with depression. She was pretty new and from out of our district. She had all the earmarks of someone who struggled. She was angry with everyone, including her parents, peers, and most of the teachers. I could not get close to her, and neither could anyone else.

One day, she had come to school in her usual down mood. I remember a teacher told me later that he noticed she had opened up a little in his class and had shared that she was "going to a better place" to some of the other kids. He thought she meant going on a trip or something like that.

Later in the afternoon, when school was out, I received a call from the police department. They sent over an officer and he told me that she had taken her life by suicide after arriving home from school.

I was in shock. While I did not really understand what was happening, I realized that I needed to do something—but I had no idea what to do. I found my custodian and asked her to clean out the girl's belongings from the locker so her locker mate would not be impacted by it. We put it all in a cardboard box.

I then talked to my psychologist and asked what he thought we should do, but he wasn't sure either. This was 1991. At the time, everyone thought it was best to "do nothing, say nothing" and hope it went by without anyone noticing. I did not even meet with the student's parents, and they did not meet with me. I had always felt like they hated the public school system because it had not gone well academically with their daughter in previous years.

I remember sitting in my office feeling sad but having no idea of what to do or how to react.

I could not believe it. Why was it acceptable that she would want to take her life? Why would someone choose suicide? Was it possible to be in so much misery that you saw no other option than to kill yourself? Something was wrong here.

Was there something we as a school system could have done differently? Was there something that I as the principal should have done? I would never know the answers from the student, but I would later learn that there are many things we as a bureaucratic educational system could and should do better.

That night, I pulled her file from the counselor's office and read the notes about her life in our public school system. In elementary school, her teachers loved her, and she was very successful. One teacher even called her a "shining star" in his fifth-grade class. Her attendance was excellent, her grades were superb, and the feedback was positive from everyone. She even won some awards in the sixth grade. Her record for the sixth grade was promising.

Then, in the seventh grade, I noticed comments from her teachers. One had written, "This student is lacking in her abilities to stay focused in my class." Another teacher said she was falling behind and not turning in her work. I wondered, *What happened in her life?*

The notes for the rest of junior high were the same. Her grades started to fall and then her attendance. There was a note about her mom angrily leaving a parent-teacher conference when a teacher blamed the mom for the problems. What was going on? What could we as a public education system have done better to help?

As I was finishing up and closing the folder, two papers fell out. One was a note from the junior high counselor reporting that she had been bullied at lunch and was found crying in the restroom by a staff member on the second day of school. The counselor met with her and was concerned about her. I did not see a follow-up with any other notes from that incident.

The other paper was a written statement from the high school hall monitor. The student had been asked to write a statement from an incident that had happened in the band room after a practice. In the note, she stated how two other girls had done a prank on her in front of the other students in the class and how the teacher had just laughed with everyone else.

Was the bullying the tip of the iceberg, or was there more? What happened from elementary to high school, and why was it so horrible for her?

How could I have helped?

I would ask myself that same question numerous times, over and over. I felt like we as a system had failed her and her family. It was sad, so sad.

Learning to Be a Principal

I was a young high school principal, and in those days, I even looked it. On Fridays, I would wear a school shirt and Levi's. One Friday, a mother who was upset about her son being suspended came to the front desk and demanded to see the principal immediately. The secretary pointed to a bench and said, "He's over there with those students."

She came to the bench and asked, "Where is the principal?" When I said I was the principal, she stormed back to the secretary and demanded to see the "real person in charge." The secretary smiled and said, "That's him."

I have been blessed to spend my career in the public school system. I believe it is one of the best equalizers for children and families. I am honored to be considered an educator and a "guardian of the children." I love kids.

During my career, I have been lucky to work with caring educators who loved children. They went the extra mile to help young people who were struggling. I was amazed at their compassion. I wish I could name them all. They taught me so much and, most importantly, they worked hard to save kids. Our school was a safe, nonthreatening environment for children because of the amazing staff.

The experienced ones taught me how to be a good educator. One such experienced educator was Virginia Swenson, who was my personal secretary. She was much older, as I was then a young principal and she had been a secretary for over forty years.

One day I caught some students breaking major school rules. I brought them into my office and chewed them out. I may have even yelled a little bit. When I was finished with them, I suspended them and told them to go call their parents. I may also have raised my voice as I showed them out of my office.

About two minutes later, Virginia stepped in while I was working at my desk. She cleared her throat to get my attention.

When I looked up, she pointed her finger at me and said, "Principals don't yell. They teach!"

I was not sure what she meant and asked for clarification. She informed me that I should not have yelled at those three kids. I disagreed and tried to defend myself. She replied again that not only should I not have yelled, but I also needed to apologize to the students.

I told her I would consider it next time. She smiled, opened the door, shuffled three repentant students back into my office, and said, "I think now is a good time to start." Then she closed the door. It was a good lesson, and it set the tone for me to be a better leader and a better listener.

She also taught me the concept of "quiet dignity," or the ability to act calm even during a heated situation. Too many times I would burst out with my frustrations at how unwise the kids could be. They would do the dumbest things and then act surprised when they got caught. To top that off, the parents would come in angry with me for their child's poor behavior. She taught me to use quiet dignity in those situations, and I was able to apply it to many similar situations during my career.

At the start of my career, I was young and inexperienced as an administrator. I was to grow old fast from dealing with suicides.

TALKING ABOUT SUICIDE

While I worked as a high school principal, I had numerous experiences with the loss of students. I spoke at funerals, comforted parents and students, and became numb to the loss of kids. It was the norm, and every year I expected to lose at least one. This, of course, did not even come close to all the attempted suicides.

I can remember one school year (181 days, 990 hours, 5.5 hours a day, 36 weeks a year) when our school district had at least one attempted suicide every week! It was hard on the families of the students and it could be difficult on the school. Most who attempted suicide did little harm to themselves. They either threw up the pills or passed out from the alcohol before they hurt themselves permanently.

Unfortunately, others hurt themselves physically and, even worse, emotionally. I learned early on that these young people did not want to die. They wanted the pain of whatever they were experiencing to go away. The suicide attempt became the mechanical arm to deal with it. Many of these attempts happened shortly after a breakup or a disciplinary action.

While I was an administrator, I learned that many young people who attempt suicide are dealing with some sort of depression. In fact, depression, alcohol or drug abuse, behavior problems, anxiety, and other mental health problems are found in about 90 percent of youth who are lost to suicide.[3] However, though many young people experience depression and other mental health issues, few will get to the point of attempting suicide because of it.

At first, it was not unusual to have a Provo police officer stop by to meet with me concerning a student who had been involved in a theft or robbery or who was having family issues. But it was becoming more common for them to stop by and visit about a student or family member who had either attempted suicide or taken his or her life by suicide.

One day, I had a visit concerning a beautiful young lady who came from the wealthy side of Provo. When I first met her mom and dad, I was impressed with their care and concern for their daughter. She was a pretty girl who had messed up at the high school and had been referred to us. When we finished meeting, the mother asked if she and I could talk privately.

I felt a little awkward as her husband went to sit outside with their daughter. The mother nervously shared that their daughter had been struggling with depression and had gotten into alcohol and serious drug problems.

She also shared that her husband was a doctor and that he had struggled with depression since medical school. She related that they were concerned about their daughter and that she had threatened to take her life numerous times. They did not know what to do. Talking with me had been their last resort.

This was becoming too common of a theme for me as a principal. Our community was full of families hurting but not wanting to admit it or even talk about it. I would experience this type of situation on a weekly basis.

One experience that showed how not talking about suicide can hurt rather than help involved a fifteen-year-old student. I was in an emergency room with her, as she had attempted to take her life. It was not a pretty situation. Her parents were scared, and she was in emotional and physical pain. The mother pulled me aside to share her fears and frustrations. She knew her daughter was struggling, but she did not know what to do.

The dad was angry and unwilling to talk about it. He just wanted to go home. I think he was hurting for his daughter, but he looked more embarrassed by the situation and frustrated with all the hospital forms and red tape. He kept asking if it would be covered by their insurance.

When I finished visiting and was ready to go, this beautiful young lady turned to me and said, "Dr. Hudnall, *I believe that my generation will be known as the generation of suicide.*" I think she was right.

Having so many experiences with students who threatened, attempted, and unfortunately died by suicide over the years, I came to understand that we as a society are afraid to talk about suicide. The subject is taboo, and we believe the myth that talking about suicide increases the risk for it.

I have come to learn that young ones who are struggling have already thought of taking their lives. In reality, however, they do not want to die. They just want the pain to go away, but they do not know how to make it go away, so they see suicide as an option.

We need to start talking about suicide, and we need to do it now, more than ever.

○ LIFESAVER ○
Talking about Suicide

We are afraid to talk about suicide. It is difficult for many people to talk about it. There is an innate fear that if we talk about it, we will give someone the idea to kill themselves.

Please do not be afraid to talk to your children. It will not put the idea of suicide in their head. There is no research to show a correlation between talking about suicide and causing a suicide. In fact, research indicates that "talking openly and responsibly about suicide lets a potentially suicidal person know they do not have to be alone. . . . Most people are relieved to finally be able to talk honestly about their feelings, and this alone can reduce the risk of an attempt."[4] In most cases, someone who is very depressed may have already thought about it. Asking will not give someone the idea.

I have found that it is helpful to talk about suicide one-on-one when you and your child are both in a good mood. Do not do it when either of you is angry or upset; it will not work. Find a time when you can meet alone with your child.

While bringing up and discussing the subject, I suggest using the "I" message as much as possible. The "I" message is a method of sharing your feelings without shaming or blaming the other person. Its use is "a way to express your own needs, expectations, problems, feelings or concerns to your children in a respectful way that does not attack them."[5]

For example, you could say, "I noticed tonight at the dinner table that you were curt with your sister. This seemed different from how you usually interact with her. Are you okay?" Then it is important to listen to what your child says. Try your best not to interrupt or give judgment. It's important for your child to know that you are really listening and not just trying to fix or judge him or her.

A few years ago, I was interviewed on KSL, Utah's statewide television station.[6] The story was about suicide in Utah and the challenges we are facing. Dave McCann, the reporter, asked difficult questions about the challenges our youth are facing in our homes, communities, churches, and schools.

At the end of the interview, he asked, "Dr. Hudnall, what do you want parents to take away from this interview?"

I replied, "I hope parents will be willing to talk to their children about their concerns with their behaviors, reactions that are not normal, and especially their fears about the child thinking of suicide."

The very next day, I received a phone call from a gentleman who asked to meet with me. At that meeting, he told me his story.

Dr. Hudnall, I want to share with you what happened with our family after watching the special on KSL television last night. My wife and I were in bed watching television when your interview came on. When you finished, my wife and I looked at each other and she said, "I think we need to talk to our son."

My son is a very talented football player, and he was injured in the state playoffs. We have been very worried about him. We know that it has affected him and will probably affect his ability to play college ball. So my wife asked me to go meet with our son right away.

I knocked on my son's door and he let me in. I walked over and sat on his bed and we visited for a little while. My son then said, "Dad, what do you want? You never come in here like this unless you want something. What's up?"

I then shared with him the interview you had on KSL, and then I said to my son, "Your mom and I are worried about you, ever since you hurt yourself. We are afraid that it has been so painful, physically and even more emotionally, that maybe you have thought about hurting yourself.

"So, son, I'm a little nervous asking you this, but Dr. Hudnall told us we need to have the courage to ask, so have you thought of hurting yourself? Have you thought of suicide?"

My son then replied, "Dad, there's no doubt that this stupid injury has been very painful. And, yes, I am afraid of not being able to play again. But, while I've been and am currently depressed, I'm not suicidal."

We hugged and then my son said, "But, Dad, I'm worried about two of my teammates. I think they are so depressed that they're thinking of killing themselves, and I'm not sure what to do."

The father went on to tell me that they talked for over an hour, and he mentioned it was one of the best discussions he and his son had had in a long time. He then informed me that he was able to reach out to the parents of the two friends, and they promised to get help for their sons.

The father then said, "Dr. Hudnall, I want to thank you for not only educating my wife and me about the challenges our kids are facing with depression but also for giving us permission to talk to our kids about suicide. It was exactly what we needed to hear. Thank you!"

CALL TO ACTION

If you have any concerns about your child or a young person you are working with, do not be afraid to ask if they have been "thinking of hurting themselves." It's also okay to ask, "Are you thinking about taking your life by suicide?"

If you are uncomfortable talking with your child, find someone else who can, maybe a grandparent, friend, clergy member, or a professional. But please, if you have any concern whatsoever, reach out and get help, and do it now!

NOTES

1. The Utah Suicide Prevention Coalition, "Data," *Utah Suicide Prevention Plan 2017–2021*, 6, accessed January 9, 2018, http://www.sprc.org/sites/default/files/UT _State%20Suicide%20Prevention%20Plan_2021.pdf.
2. "Suicide: Utah 2017 Facts & Figures," American Foundation for Suicide Prevention, accessed January 9, 2018, https://afsp.org/about-suicide/state-fact-sheet/#Utah.
3. "Teen Suicide Statistics," American Academy of Pediatrics, updated October 18, 2016, https://www.healthychildren.org/English/health-issues/conditions/emotional-problems /Pages/Teen-Suicide-Statistics.aspx.
4. "FAQs about Suicide," Crisis Centre, accessed January 9, 2018, https://crisiscentre .bc.ca/frequently-asked-questions-about-suicide.
5. "The Skill of I-Messages—What to Say When We Are Upset," The Center for Parenting Education, accessed January 6, 2018, https://centerforparentingeducation.org/library-of -articles/healthy-communication/the-skill-of-i-messages-what-to-say-when-we-are-upset.
6. The interview can be found at https://www.ksl.com/?nid=960&sid=24939059&title =how-to-talk-about-suicide-with-your-youth.

CHAPTER 2

It Takes Everyone
to Save Lives

Suicide is real. To those of you who have experienced its effects and become part of a family that no one wants to be part of, I am sorry for your loss. Only the mother, the father, the sibling, and other family members can really understand what it means to lose a child to suicide. Though I was not related to these students, as their principal I saw and felt a part of the pain from their loss.

One suicide that stands out happened early on and was very painful. To this day I wonder if I could have done a better job recognizing the warning signs and reaching out to help. It is something that still haunts me, as most of them do.

I had a student who was one of those kids you either loved or hated. He came from a tough background and had a father who did not put up with nonsense. His father had high expectations for his son and two daughters.

I came to know the family through numerous home visits and even from time in court for the boy's truancy. My student wasn't lazy or stupid; he was just bored. He liked to sneak out of school and have a smoke. We caught him numerous times, and his mom or dad would come in each time, and we would have interesting discussions on what to do to help their son.

He finally found some success in his junior year and started to make progress. His grades got better, his attendance improved, and he was hitting his stride. One time we discussed the idea of him going to our local vocational college to become a mechanic. As he settled down, he became popular and even had his first steady girlfriend. They went everywhere together.

Then one night I received a call from his father. He asked if I would come to the hospital right away. His son was in a coma on life support, and they did not think he would make it. I found out that he had been in a fight with his girlfriend. They had an argument and he had threatened to kill himself if she did not come back to him. But she was tired of his games and told him to take a hike. He then tried to take his life by suicide. At the hospital, the family was advised to pull the plug, and he died.

Once again, a suicide devastated the entire school community. I think I cried for a week.

PREVENTING SUICIDE INVOLVES EVERYONE

A year later, I convinced my school board, my superintendent, and my staff that we should be one of the first year-round high schools in the country. We lost many kids academically during summer; it was too long of a break from school for students who struggle. Going year-round gave us more time to interact with them and provide academic and emotional support.

For the year-round school, we developed a unique schedule. The school year was 180 days divided into four sections of forty-five days "on" (in school) and fifteen days out of school, with five days of what we called "Intersession" (out of school, but still together).

We decided to include camping trips in those five days "off," because it was a way to take the kids somewhere without spending a lot of money on hotels. We also performed a lot of service that allowed the kids to grow emotionally as they forgot about their problems and focused on others. We wrote a grant and received funding for vans, trailers, tents, sleeping bags, Dutch ovens, and everything else you needed to take one hundred kids out into the wilderness of Utah.

My fellow administrators thought I was crazy, and, to be honest, I probably was. Every forty-five days I was off for five to ten days with about sixty kids. We traveled to Zion National Park (Utah), Canada, Washington, and California, and every spring we spent time on the Navajo reservation doing service projects. My assistant principal, Judy, put it all together. She was the expert who made it happen. It was a lot of work, but it also helped us pull together as a school.

One school year, we were out for a high school senior overnighter. We had the local television news with us, filming our activities. We were out on a lake in canoes when one of the students returned to the cabin to go to the restroom. As soon as she entered the cabin, she came right back out, screaming that a fellow student had attempted suicide and was on the floor, foaming at the mouth.

I ran to the cabin. With the help of Judy, Pat (my PTA president), and a college intern, we got the student into the bathroom and poured ipecac down his throat. I was standing with one foot in the bathtub and one foot out, holding the student over the toilet. He would throw up and then I would throw up (I gag anytime someone throws up). He had swallowed a bottle of Tylenol.

We called the hospital back in our community, which was two hours away. The emergency room doctor said, "Principal, you have to get that kid down here right away. And do whatever you have to do, but don't let him fall asleep, as it may shut down his internal organs." When I hung up, I thought, *What the heck am I going to do?*

I told Judy to take over watching the other students. Then I asked the college intern if she could drive her car, and I asked Pat to jump in the back of the car and hold a garbage bag for the student to throw up in. There was no way I was going to be able to do it, so I decided to sit in the front.

The car was a little one with not much room. The college intern was scared to death, as was I. We sped down the mountain road. Every so often, Pat would yell, "Greg, he's falling asleep!" I would turn in my seat and slap him in the face. He would wake up and together we would throw up in the bag.

By the time we drove to the Provo emergency room, my hand was swollen to three times its normal size. I could not even bend my fingers. The emergency team came running out, put the student on a gurney, and ran him into the hospital.

As the three of us were crying and hoping he would make it, a large man walked up, introduced himself as the student's father, and asked what had happened. He said that he had just come from the hospital and his son's face was really swollen. Everyone looked at me, and I quietly put my hand behind my back and said, "I'm not sure, but it appears that he had fallen when he swallowed the pills." I was scared I would be in trouble.

When we later met with the medical team and I shared our story with the doctor, he said, "Principal, you probably saved his life!"

If it had not been for my PTA president, an intern, and, most of all, the fellow student who found the boy, we may have lost him to suicide. I was beginning to learn that it takes all of us to prevent a suicide.

Two weeks after the incident, I was required to attend an "Executive Session" with my school board members and my superintendent to review what had happened. To be honest, I was scared. Aside from when I was hired, I had yet to meet with the entire school board, except during the yearly review where all the principals met.

The superintendent was a kind, supportive person. He believed in allowing his principals to try new things to help kids succeed. When he called and informed me that I would need to come prepared to discuss in detail what had happened with the attempted suicide, I asked, "Am I in trouble?"

He replied that he did not think so, but he assured me that he would do all that he could to help me. He ended the phone call by saying, "Greg, please don't ever be afraid to try to help kids."

We met in the board conference room. There were seven board members, the superintendent, his assistant, and the director of secondary education. I was asked to describe what happened, what we did to intervene, and what we could have done to prevent it.

For twenty minutes, I shared our story and how everyone was involved. Two of the board members asked especially probing questions. It was scary, and at times I even doubted myself. The question that kept rising to the top was, "Principal Hudnall, you took sixty of the most difficult kids into the wilderness and allowed this to happen. Why would we as a school district let you keep doing this?"

Toward the end, one of the board members asked the superintendent a tough question: "Should Principal Hudnall be disciplined for his lack of preparation for or understanding of what could have happened?"

I was frozen in my seat. I thought about how I had been a principal for only a few years and was already in trouble. I also wondered if I was naïve to think that we would never have any problems with the program.

The superintendent sat for a moment and then replied, "We lose kids to suicide in every secondary school in this district. Last year we lost two students from other schools. This is not a new phenomenon. We as a district need to have the courage to support Principal Hudnall. We must have the courage to find ways to help these kids who are struggling. If we punish an administrator who is trying to help, we might as well give up."

The school board president interjected, "I agree!" Within a few seconds, everyone agreed. The board president closed the meeting by saying, "Principal Hudnall, we as a board appreciate all that you're doing. We do not find fault and instead encourage you to continue what you're doing to save these kids' lives."

That message would resonate with me for my next twenty-five years with the school district.

This experience, along with others, helped me realize that even "less obvious" people play an important part in suicide prevention. As a school principal, I assumed that the two most important people on campus for dealing with mental health issues or preventing a suicide were the principal (administrator) and the school counselor. But I came to learn that the two most important people in my school were the lunch lady and the custodian. They were not disciplinarians, so students would open up to them.

My custodian was loved by the students. She was always helping them with a jammed locker or a flat tire. They saw her as kind and supportive. Over time, they would open up to her.

The other most important person was one of the lunch ladies. I would go down to the lunchroom to check on students and make sure there weren't any food fights or other issues. The lunch ladies knew the names of every student. As students went through the lunch line, this lunch lady would give an extra dessert to students who were struggling.

Over time, the custodian and the lunch lady began to come into my office to express concerns about specific kids. I loved it. It helped me understand the importance of having all staff involved with that part of suicide prevention—knowing the warning signs and knowing how to talk to struggling students.

You never know who students will connect with. For example, kids could open up to a teacher they love and respect. That teacher needs to know and understand the warning signs of suicide, how to talk to a struggling student, and when to involve the school counselor.

Because many youths give warning signs or make comments before attempting suicide, it is important for everyone to know and be able to recognize warning signs in others.

○ LIFESAVER ○
Warning Signs

It is important to understand that risk factors and warning signs are very different. While risk factors are aspects of someone's life that make them more susceptible or more at risk for suicide, warning signs are new developments in someone's life that point to them being at immediate risk for suicide.[1] Risk factors will be covered later in the book.

Common warning signs include the following:

1. Talking about or making plans for suicide.
2. Expressing hopelessness about the future.
3. Displaying severe/overwhelming emotional pain or distress.
4. Showing worrisome behavioral cues or marked changes in behavior, particularly in the presence of the warning signs above. Specifically, this includes significant
   ○ withdrawal from or changing in social connections/situations.
   ○ changes in sleep (increased or decreased).
   ○ anger or hostility that seems out of character or out of context.
   ○ recent increased agitation or irritability.[2]

CALL TO ACTION

If you notice any of these warning signs in others, take the following actions:

1. Ask if they are ok or if they are having thoughts of suicide.
2. Express your concern about what you are observing in their behavior.
3. Listen attentively and non-judgmentally.
4. Reflect what they share and let them know they have been heard.
5. Tell them they are not alone.
6. Let them know there are treatments available that can help.
7. If you are or they are concerned, guide them to additional professional help.[3]

As they receive help, continue to support and reach out to them in love and acceptance.

NOTES

1. Suicide Prevention Resource Center and Philip Rogers, "Understanding Risk and Protective Factors for Suicide: A Primer for Preventing Suicide" (Newton, MA: Education Development Center, Inc., 2011), accessed January 9, 2018, https://www .sprc.org/sites/default/files/migrate/library/RiskProtectiveFactorsPrimer.pdf.
2. "Youth Suicide Warning Signs," *Youth Suicide Warning Signs*, accessed January 9, 2018, http://www.youthsuicidewarningsigns.org/healthcare-professionals. (The information provided on the website comes from a collaboration of expert panelists in Rockville, Maryland, in 2013, held by leaders from the American Association of Suicidology, the National Center for Prevention of Youth Suicide, and the Substance Abuse and Mental Health Services Administration. A complete list of all the panelists who participated can be found at youthsuicidewarningsigns.org/about.)
3. "Youth Suicide Warning Signs," *Youth Suicide Warning Signs*.

CHAPTER 3

A Meaningful Funeral Talk

The next year, we had a junior who had been in and out of trouble. He had a girlfriend, and the two went everywhere together. One night they had a fight, and he got into his dad's gun closet and tried to take his life.

The shot went through his mouth and out his eye. He was alive when they found him. He was in the hospital for three months. When I finally had a chance to meet with him, I asked him what had happened.

He said, "My girlfriend and I had been fighting for a few weeks, and it was getting worse. I knew she was going to break up with me. Well, she did. On Thursday night after the ball game, she broke up with me. I was so distraught and in so much pain.

"I began to drink, and then I figured that if I killed myself on Friday, she would feel so bad over the weekend that we would be back together on Monday." Then he looked over at me with scars on his face and said, "I guess I messed that one up, didn't I?"

He would never be the same.

WANTING THE PAIN TO GO AWAY

Over time, I have come to realize that kids do not want to die. They want the pain to go away. At that moment, they are hurting so bad that they cannot feel or see their way out of it. So suicide becomes an option. I came to call it the "24/48"-hour crisis. Something happens that triggers that emotion, the pain is real for them, and then they try to find a way to deal with it.

Unfortunately, these young people do not have the capacity at that moment to deal with the crisis. In many situations, the stress they are dealing with exceeds their coping ability, and in most cases the young person is suffering from a mental health condition. Suicide appeals to them at that painful time. They want the pain to stop and are willing to do anything, including hurting themselves, to make it go away.

One time I was sitting with a group of students and watching our school basketball team play. One of the students who was sitting off by himself had been struggling the last few days, and I was worried about him. He was not a bad kid—just lost. He seemed to be acting differently. He was angry with everyone around him and one teacher told me he "snapped" at her over some silly thing.

He was in tenth grade and around sixteen years old. I scooted closer to him and casually asked, "How are you doing?"

He replied, "I'm fine."

After a few minutes, I responded with, "I'm worried about you. I noticed that you were struggling in some of your classes and that you haven't been hanging out with your group of friends. What's up?"

He actually teared up and said, "I'm fine, Greg [what my students called me]. Just let it be," as he wiped the tears away.

I knew something was wrong. Being the nosy principal that I was, I moved closer to him so no one else would hear us. I then asked, "How can I help?"

After a few minutes of staring into space, he shared his personal story with me. His story made me tear up. When he finished, I was able to get him to our school counselor, who helped direct him to professional services in our community.

This was to become my method of operation. I would recognize someone struggling and in a private moment pull him or her aside and ask how he or she was doing.

After many failed conversations with students, I learned to use the "I" message whenever I spoke to a student who was struggling. It was less threatening and showed that I cared about them. I always asked, "How can I help?"

LEARNING A LESSON ABOUT LIFE

The next school year, our school administrative team was invited by the US Department of Education to present in Dallas, Texas. We had received a grant for funding to work with at-risk kids and their families. We were having a lot of success, so they invited us to the national conference.

My whole administrative team went with me, including an administrative intern named Tim. It was a four-day event, and we were enjoying interacting and learning from fellow educators. On day two, my superintendent called and said, "Principal Hudnall, you better get back here as soon as possible. You lost a student to suicide this morning and there is concern that you may lose one or two more!"

I turned to Tim and asked him to arrange to get me home while I started packing. I asked Judy, my assistant principal, to take over while I headed home to see what I could do to help.

I remember packing and thinking, *I am not sure I can keep going through this.* A few minutes later, Tim stepped in and said, "They'll have a car for you in a few minutes." I grabbed my suitcase and headed for the entrance.

When I got downstairs to the front lobby, the concierge said, "Mr. Hudnall, the limo is waiting for you. Is everything okay?" I told him we would be fine and headed out the door to a huge black limo. The driver had the door open for me and grabbed my bags. I had never been in a limo before.

When we got to the airport, I was escorted from the limo to the ticket counter by two security guards and an escort. I kept thinking I was in trouble. The ticket agent at the counter was so nice. She had my ticket ready for me and asked if I was okay. I told her I was a little shaken and she almost teared up. I thought, *Wow, these people are so caring and supportive about my poor student.*

I was walked to the plane in front of everyone else and put in first class. I had never flown first class before. As I was sitting in the huge, comfortable seat, a flight attendant came over to me with some wine. She leaned over and asked, "Would you like a drink?" When I declined (as I do not drink), she said, "Oh, of course, you are on duty. Please accept my apology."

The experience getting home was weird, although I can tell you that first class is very roomy and a great way to fly. A few weeks later, the grant director called from DC and asked how the funeral went. When I shared how strange the trip getting home was, he just laughed.

He then informed me that in DC, the departments sometimes share funds when it is close to the year-end budget time. If they have too much money left, they not only lose that funding, but they will also have it deducted from the next year's budget. My travel funds came from some other budget associated with a security budget. They thought I was an important person flying to protect someone.

When I got home, the impact of the suicide in our community was devastating. I visited with the family and once again was asked to speak at the funeral. Because of the way the students reacted to it, this funeral affected me differently than the other funerals.

There were hundreds of kids crying over the casket. They were weeping, shouting, and hugging each other as they came through the viewing line. I did not even know the student well. He had not been in my office, nor had my assistant dealt with him. He was not on our radar screen as someone to worry about, although later one of my counselors reminded me that at times it felt like we were worried about everyone for some reason or another.

This student had gotten in trouble with the law. While I never knew all the details, I was aware that he was struggling with serious charges and would likely be going to the juvenile detention center.

By this time, I had spoken at three or four funerals and had a funeral talk already prepared. All I needed to do was to add the student's name. As I was preparing for the funeral, however, I had a spiritual feeling that I needed to throw the talk away and give a new one. To this day, I am not sure why, but I did. I spoke on love, tolerance, and forgiveness.

This funeral taught me a good lesson about how life can be difficult for some but even more challenging for others. The message in my talk seemed to resonate with everyone else there too. I also mentioned that I thought it was important not to judge, but to be more kind and more caring with one another. I think the talk helped me as much as it did those in the audience. When the funeral was over, a few of the student's friends greeted me, and we hugged and shared their pain.

After the funeral, I sat in the background, watching the many kids who were struggling with their friend's death. Many were angry, but most were just hurting from the loss.

I realized that this was not a bad kid. In fact, I had very few bad kids in my school. This was once again a child who was lost and trying to find himself. He got in with tough kids who had accepted him in a time of need, and he was soon pulled into their lifestyle.

While I did not know the student very well, I did know his family. They were good people who were trying their best. After the funeral, the father thanked me for my short words of wisdom. As I listened to him, I could feel his pain. He had his hand on my shoulder as he was thanking me. His wife was off to the side, holding their daughter, and both were sobbing.

I asked, "How are you doing?"

He started to shake and then he broke down. We put our arms around each other and just cried. He cried for the loss of a child he loved and would miss the rest of his life.

I cried for him, his family, his son—and even more as a father. While I could not experience the pain firsthand, I could understand the pain as a father who loved his children. I cannot even imagine how bad it would feel to lose a child.

Once again, I had this feeling that we needed to do more to prevent these kids from killing themselves. But what? My challenge was to figure out why suicide happens and how to help those struggling. It would take me years to find the complete answer.

Part of the answer involves protective factors, which are "personal or environmental characteristics that help protect people from suicide."[1] Knowing these protective factors can help prevent mental, emotional, and behavioral disorders that may increase someone's risk for suicide.

Another part of the answer is to promote resiliency in your child's life. Resiliency is "an ability to recover from or adjust easily to misfortune or change."[2] Childhood can be difficult, and building resiliency in our children is critical to their success in life. They learn how to deal with difficulty instead of resorting to drastic actions such as suicide.

✪ LIFESAVER ✪
Protective Factors
and Resiliency

The first question that parents always ask me is, "What can I do to prevent my child from thinking of hurting himself?" The following protective factors[3] are personal characteristics that are critical to helping your child, and these characteristics also help children build resiliency.

Effective Behavioral Health Care

One of the key parts of suicide prevention is making sure that anyone at risk for suicide has access to effective care. Elements of this access include availability of treatment, levels of care, and timely follow-ups and referrals.[4]

Connectedness

Connectedness is "the degree to which a person or group is socially close, interrelated, or shares resources with other persons or groups."[5] As a high school principal, I found that connectedness was one of the most important factors for young people. It did not matter if it was sports, performing arts, afterschool programs, music, or even volunteering—I found that children who have friends and are connected to something or someone had better attendance, higher grades, better behavior, and higher self-esteem.

Having connections in family, community, and social institutions lends support, which is especially important for struggling children. But it is also important to remember that not all social connections are healthy.

One of the top things families can do is to have at least one meal a day together. Leave the cell phones and the television off. Take time to connect!

Another way to develop positive connections is to create opportunities to make and keep friends by attending community events, participating in recreational activities, or inviting your child's peers to your home. For our kids, my wife used one night of the week as "friend night," where our children could invite kids over for various activities and to eat treats and pizza. Friends are also important because they allow your children to learn new things and to share things that they may not share with an adult or family member.

Kids who feel alone may have a higher risk for depression, so a connection to peers is critical. If your child likes to be alone, find ways for them to connect in a healthy, nonthreatening way. Teach your child empathy and how to be a friend; this will make them more likely to know how to make friends.

If you homeschool, find ways to interact with other homeschool families. In Utah, homeschoolers may be able to have their children participate in extra-curricular activities with the schools. Look at your community recreation pro-gram or after-school programs. There are a lot of resources out there. Do not be afraid to ask for help from school leaders, community partners, and others.

Find out what works best for you and your family. We have made many mistakes along the way, but we keep trying. A parent of a struggling student had his child try numerous activities to see what interested her. In the end, it was chess, and her parents signed her up for a community chess club. The dad said it was the best thing he could have done.

Self-Esteem and a Sense of Purpose or Meaning in Life

Self-esteem can be defined as what we think about ourselves. It is the confi-dence we have in ourselves or how happy we are with ourselves. Those with a sense of purpose or meaning feel motivated and inspired to go about life. People with these qualities are much less likely to commit suicide, because they know how to deal with difficult situations.

Another way you can help is to teach your child to help others. This empow-ers them and provides them with a purpose. Also enlist their help around the house with appropriate chores. Praise them for their help and effort.

One way to help with self-esteem is to teach your child about the impor-tance of having a well-balanced diet, exercising regularly, and getting enough sleep. All these factors can help your child feel good in mind and body.

Cultural, Religious, or Personal Beliefs That Discourage Suicide

Utah has been in the top ten states for suicide for the past twenty years. Because Utah is known for its large population of Mormons, or members of The Church of Jesus Christ of Latter-day Saints, many people ask me about the "Mormon" impact on suicide. They ask if belonging to the Mormon church increases the risk for suicide.

Interestingly enough, religion is a resiliency factor, regardless of the religion, because of the connectedness factor. It also increases resiliency when religious leaders discourage suicide, like the Mormon church does.

These protective factors can build resiliency in your child and protect your child from risk factors he or she may have.[6]

CALL TO ACTION

Use the above suggestions to encourage resiliency in your child's life and continually build on your relationship with your children. A good relationship will put you in a better position to recognize when your child is struggling, and it will enable you to build a level of trust so the child will feel comfortable to come to you when he or she is struggling. The following ideas[7] will help you cultivate a good relationship with your children:

- Eat one meal together as a family without television or electronic devices.
- Give your child a home environment that is safe both physically and emotionally.
- Spend quality time with your child.
- Listen carefully to what your child says and anything he or she might be trying to convey.
- Be supportive without being intrusive.
- Encourage your child to express positive and negative emotion.

Doing these things can put you in a perfect position to help suicide prevention. A close relationship helps you intervene in your child's stressful situations, detect possible mental illness early, and track suicide warning signs such as drastic changes in behavior.[8]

NOTES

1. "Risk and Protective Factors," Suicide Prevention Resource Center, accessed January 19, 2018, https://www.sprc.org/about-suicide/risk-protective-factors.
2. "Resilient," *Merriam-Webster.com*, accessed March 5, 2018.
3. Adapted from a list found at "Risk and Protective Factors," Suicide Prevention Resource Center.
4. "Ensure Access to Effective Care and Treatment," Suicide Prevention Resource Center, accessed January 19, 2018, https://www.sprc.org/comprehensive-approach/effective-care.
5. "Strategic Direction for the Prevention of Suicidal Behavior: Promoting Individual, Family, and Community Connectedness to Prevent Suicidal Behavior," Centers for Disease Control and Prevention, accessed January 19, 2018, https://www.cdc.gov /ViolencePrevention/pdf/Suicide_Strategic_Direction_Full_Version-a.pdf.

6. "Promote Social Connectedness and Support," Suicide Prevention Resource Center, accessed January 19, 2018, https://www.sprc.org/comprehensive-approach/social-connectedness.

7. Adapted from information found at "What Can Parents Do to Prevent Youth Suicides?" Nevada Division of Public and Behavioral Health: Office of Suicide Prevention, accessed January 20, 2018, http://suicideprevention.nv.gov/Youth/WhatYouCanDo.

8. "What Can Parents Do to Prevent Youth Suicides?" Nevada Division of Public and Behavioral Health: Office of Suicide Prevention.

CHAPTER 4

Relationships Are Key to Suicide Prevention

After a few years at the helm, my superintendent retired. I enjoyed working with him, and I felt that he would always be there if I needed to go to him for help. He had high expectations of me and expected nothing but the best, but he did it in a way that was supportive and complimentary. He was the first of six superintendents I would work for during my years in the Provo City School District.

He was replaced by one of my colleagues, a principal from one of the other high schools. The new superintendent was a nice guy, but he did not like to be bothered. He once said to me, "Principal Hudnall, your job is to get those kids graduated."

The pressure for high graduation rates was intense because the rates were one of the top indicators for a successful superintendent. He did not talk much, and, to be honest, I was afraid to go to him for help. Nevertheless, I kept pursuing suicide prevention the best I could.

During this time, we were raising our children on a farm in southwest Provo. At night, my wife had the phone next to her side of the bed. One Friday night early in the school year, at about one thirty a.m., the phone rang. My heart started racing.

My wife picked it up, and as she did, we both heard loud voices swearing and calling me names. She listened for a moment and, not saying a word to the caller, handed me the phone. She said, "It's for you." She then turned over and went back to sleep.

I had suspended some students that day, and it appeared that they were still angry over it. I listened for a few minutes and then told them to stop calling me, stop drinking, and find someone to drive them home. As I was hanging up, I said, "Brian and Jeff, don't call again." They were surprised I recognized their voices. I chuckled and went back to sleep.

I could take a phone call like that anytime. It was the possibility that the call was going to be about the loss of a student that made me afraid to answer the phone. It happened at all times of the day and on all days of the week.

LOSING LIVES TO DEPRESSION

One challenge was that it wasn't only children who were taking their lives. Provo also lost adults to suicide. Unfortunately, some of these adults were the parents of my students, and this had a huge impact on the family members.

I remember meeting with a mother about concerns with her daughter. The student had said some things to a friend in class, and the art teacher had heard her talking about not wanting to live anymore. The teacher brought it to my attention, so a school counselor and I met with her and, having enough concerns, invited the mother to come in and visit with us as well.

The mother shared that her husband had taken his life by suicide two years earlier. As she sobbed and we tried to comfort her, she informed us that her husband's uncle had taken his life by suicide three or four years earlier and that the uncle's father had attempted suicide years before.

She said the family struggled with severe depression and that her husband's sister had been in the state hospital for years. The mother was afraid of losing her oldest daughter, who at age fourteen was outside the office, wanting to die. To be honest, I felt scared for the family, and I was just an outsider.

What do you say or do to help a family in a situation like this? For me, it was all hands on deck with our school staff and outside resources. For some reason, everyone thinks the schools can fix everything, and for some reason, the schools want everyone else to fix everything.

One of the best things I learned from this experience was that there is no one solution, nor is there a quick fix, for students and families struggling with a mental illness.

IDENTIFYING PROBLEMS THROUGH PARENT-TEACHER CONFERENCES

I remember a meeting with my fellow principals where we talked about parent-teacher conferences. In the elementary schools, an average of 70 to 80 percent of parents were coming in to meet with the teachers. Parents of struggling kids wanted to know how to help. Even parents who did not speak English would come in and ask how to help their children. The elementary principals loved it and said it felt like they were all one family.

The junior high principals talked about averaging 35 to 40 percent parental attendance at parent-teacher conferences. In many instances, they would have parents from both ends—the kids who struggled and the kids who had high performance. Both sets would want to know how to help and intervene.

The high school principals shared that they were lucky to have 19 to 25 percent of their parents attend parent-teacher conferences. And, unfortunately, most of the parents who were coming in to visit the teachers were concerned that their child was only averaging a 96 percent in their class. The parents of kids struggling and failing very rarely came in to visit their children's teachers.

The more I looked into it, the more I realized that we were as much the problem as the parents. We make parents line up for hours and then rush them through a short visit. It is unfortunate. As a principal, we did different things to help, but it was still not enough.

Parent-teacher conferences were important to us as educators, because we could use them to develop a rapport with parents and share concerns. Asking questions also helped us understand the parents' perspective better.

When parents would not come to parent-teacher conferences, we missed out on opportunities to further understand the students and we also missed out on opportunities for parent-teacher collaboration. Parent-teacher conferences were often the only way we could visit with parents.

One of the first things I try to help parents understand about youth suicide prevention is the importance of close relationships between children and adults. It's important to get to know your kids when they are young. With social media, cyberbullying, and other challenges, kids need an adult who will help them navigate unchartered waters.

One way to have a close relationship with your children is to become involved and supportive in different facets of their lives. In this way, parent-teacher conferences could play an important role in suicide prevention. They allow teachers and parents to collaborate on student risk factors: "characteristics that make it more likely that individuals will consider, attempt, or die by suicide."[1] Knowing risk factors can help teachers and parents look for possible suicide warning signs.

○ LIFESAVER ○
RISK FACTORS

Unlike warning signs, risk factors show that a person is at a higher risk for suicide than a person who doesn't have these factors; it does not mean a person is in immediate danger of suicide. Increasing the number of protective factors helps combat existing risk factors.

Major risk factors for suicide include

○ Prior suicide attempt(s)
○ Misuse and abuse of alcohol or other drugs

○ Mental disorders, particularly depression and other mood disorders
○ Access to lethal means
○ Knowing someone who died by suicide, particularly a family member
○ Social isolation
○ Chronic disease and disability
○ Lack of access to behavioral health care[2]

Risk factors can vary depending on age group, culture, gender, and other characteristics. Examples of these are stress from bullying or family rejection among lesbian, gay, bisexual, and transgender (LGBT) youth, historical trauma of American Indians and Alaska Natives, and, for middle-aged men, stressors such as unemployment and divorce.[3]

CALL TO ACTION

Make a list of protective factors and risk factors for your child. If your child has a lot more risk factors than protective factors, you should be concerned.[4] One of the biggest risk factors is if your child has had a prior suicide attempt. Someone who has attempted suicide is much more likely to be at risk for suicide than someone who has not attempted it.[5]

After a training session, I will invariably have parents come up to me and share that their child has attempted suicide but seems fine. I always ask them to have their child seen by a professional mental health expert. I explain that although their child may be fine at that time, the child could again struggle and not know what to do. Being seen by an expert long term may help your child in the long run.

NOTES

1. Suicide Prevention Resource Center and Philip Rogers, "Understanding Risk and Protective Factors for Suicide: A Primer for Preventing Suicide" (Newton, MA: Education Development Center, Inc., 2011), accessed January 9, 2018, https://www .sprc.org/sites/default/files/migrate/library/RiskProtectiveFactorsPrimer.pdf.
2. "Risk and Protective Factors," Suicide Prevention Resource Center, accessed January 19, 2018, https://www.sprc.org/about-suicide/risk-protective-factors.
3. "Risk and Protective Factors," Suicide Prevention Resource Center.
4. Nadine Kaslow, "Teen Suicides: What Are the Risk Factors?" Child Mind Institute, accessed January 20, 2018, https://childmind.org/article/teen-suicides-risk-factors.
5. David Owens, Judith Horrocks, and Allan House, "Fatal and Non-Fatal Repetition of Self-Harm: Systematic Review," *British Journal of Psychiatry* 181, no. 3 (2002): 193–99, http://bjp.rcpsych.org/content/181/3/193.long.

CHAPTER 5

Time for a Change

I had been the principal for twelve years. We had designed and built a brand-new school and had won numerous awards and recognition from around the country. At one point, I was considered one of the top administrators working with at-risk kids.

And yet, at times, I felt like a failure.

I could have amazing attendance records, set new graduation rates, and see kids go on to college, but all that is nothing when you lose a student to suicide. It haunted me that I could not save these kids from hurting themselves.

One suicide in particular still haunts me. In 1999, the local police called and asked me if I would be willing to come down to Paul Ream Wilderness Park, a public park located by my high school. They needed my help identifying the body of a fourteen-year-old who had taken his life by suicide. It was by far one of the most challenging experiences I have ever had to deal with.

One of the officers on site was incredibly kind and supportive. He asked me if I would be okay. I told him I thought so. When we finished, I walked to my car, leaned against it, threw up, and sobbed.

When I could finally get myself together, I sat in my car and cried some more and became angry. I was angry with this young man, who had so much life ahead of him. I was angry with myself for not being able to save him. I was angry at a society where youth suicide had become so prevalent. What was happening?

I thought of his wonderful family, who had raised an amazing young man, and of how they would suffer the rest of their lives. I was hurting, but I could never imagine the pain that they would suffer. Why? Why would such a young person see suicide as an option?

The longer I sat, the more I wondered what he had been struggling with. I did not understand mental illness, nor could I imagine how someone so young could be in so much pain. Whatever it was, there had to be a way to intervene early enough to help prevent this from happening all over again.

I was feeling helpless. I had lost one too many young kids to suicide. How could I as a caring, involved administrator allow this to happen? This was on my watch and was my responsibility. I loved these kids, many as if they were my own. I visited their homes, ate meals with their families, and went to church with them. How could this be happening in my community? I had failed again, and at that moment I felt utterly hopeless and helpless. I cried with such anguish, such pain. I sat in my car for a long time.

While I was sitting in my car, one of the ambulance drivers who had helped load the body and knew me came over to my car and asked if I was okay. I told him I was fine, but we both knew I wasn't.

As I wiped away the tears and resolved the anger, I made a vow. I promised that I would do all that I could to prevent the next young person from taking his or her life. I did not know how, but I knew something had to be done.

CHANGING JOBS

Within a short period of time after that incident, the assistant superintendent retired. The position was posted, and I was encouraged to apply. The current superintendent was relatively new and was from out of state. He was a kind and supportive leader. I felt like it would be a good move for me to work with him.

I was worn out from being a high school administrator. Beside all the usual job-description responsibilities, I was dealing with suicide all the time, but I didn't feel like I was doing enough.

Everywhere I went, someone would ask me about the latest suicide. I would hear about it at the grocery store, at church meetings, and even at the ballpark. I could tell people were as frustrated and worn out as I was. Our school resource officer told me that, as a police system, they were dealing with more deaths than ever, and that for every suicide, there were ten times as many attempts.

At this point, I had been working at the high school level for almost fifteen years. I had probably grown as much as I could academically and emotionally. While I loved being with the kids, I could tell I was wearing out everyone, including myself. It was time for a change.

Change at a school is difficult. In fairness to the teachers and everyone else, I would start a new program and then, when I could tell it was not working, I would want to start something else. In fact, one of my former teachers told me he was glad I was leaving the high school because I had unrealistic expectations and made too many changes. It was driving the teachers and the union crazy.

I am a change agent. When I see something that does not work, I want to fix it. But change is difficult when you work within a large bureaucracy like a school system. Leaving the high school was a challenge because, as the principal, you're in charge of everything. At the district, this wouldn't be the case. Change was going to be difficult, but at least I thought I could make things happen.

I was to find out that things did not change as easily at the top as I had thought.

✪ LIFESAVER ✪
Coping and Problem-Solving Skills

Whenever I do suicide prevention training for educators, I end up with dozens of elementary teachers sharing stories about students dealing with anxiety, depression, and other serious mental health issues. The teachers would often share concerns about the increase in the number of younger children dealing with these serious issues.

These stories are concerning, because those who have a hard time coping with or solving problems could be at a higher risk for suicide than those who do not have those problems.[1] I have seen young people who have chosen to react to situations by using suicide because they couldn't cope with stress or their situation and didn't see any other options. Developing strong coping and problem-solving skills at a young age could help these children to better handle stress or hard situations.

One example of how kids develop coping skills came while I worked with a top-notch elementary principal. We would walk into a class of thirty students, and within a few minutes she could pick out the kids who were likely to fail or struggle their entire time in school.

When I asked how she knew it so clearly, she replied, "They have a tough time coping with change and have poor problem-solving skills."

Later, I was assigned to work with one of our inner-city elementary school administrators. Her goal was to find ways to implement coping and problem-solving skills into the daily routine of classwork. She did it with dual immersion classes, where kids speak two languages—one language one day and the other language the next day.

To be honest, I was skeptical of how well it would work. It seemed like there were too many challenges, but I was proven wrong within a short period of time. With the right support and a caring faculty, these kids rose to the top. They were challenged and supported and even expected to succeed, and they did!

Language-coping skills helped these students get through the daily challenges of change. It was impressive, and they would be able to use the same coping skills for everyday life. Developing these skills helps children during stressful situations or crises because the children are able to use resources, internal and external, to maneuver successfully and positively through the situation.[2]

CALL TO ACTION

There are many sites for ideas on how to help your children learn coping and problem-solving skills. One helpful article that I like to refer parents to is from the *Therapy Changes* blog, which outlines eight steps parents can take to teach problem-solving skills to their children. The eight steps are as follows:

1. Encourage creativity.
2. Have patience.
3. Play problem-solving games.
4. Model.
5. Allow them to fail.
6. Ask for their help.
7. Propose multiple possibilities.
8. Praise their efforts vs. the result.[3]

I encourage you to find the websites and articles that you feel most comfortable with and use them to help your children develop critical coping and problem-solving skills.

NOTES

1. Sonia Chehil and Stan Kutcher, "Suicide Risk Management: A Manual for Health Professionals," 2nd ed. (West Sussex, UK; John Wiley & Sons, 2012), 48.
2. Chehil and Kutcher, "Suicide Risk Management: A Manual for Health Professionals."
3. This list comes from a blog post written by Jennifer Wendt, "8 Steps to Help Your Child Learn Problem Solving Skills," *Therapy Changes*, posted March 4, 2016, http://therapychanges.com/blog/2016/03/8-steps-child-learn-problem-solving-skills.

PART 2

The District Office: Change Can Be Difficult

CHAPTER 6

A Tough Opportunity

In the weeks leading up to my interview for the assistant superintendent position, I worked hard to prepare my presentation. I put together a ten-page proposal of things I felt needed to change to support schools and families better across the district.

I outlined changes to our suspension and expulsion policy, I rewrote the attendance policy, and I outlined how we would work with kids struggling with drug addictions. I outlined opportunities for community collaborations and partnerships. I also created a proposal for working in partnership with city leaders (made easier because the Provo City School District was a one-city school, so we needed approval by only one mayor and one city council).

During my interview, instead of focusing on the basics of curriculum, I presented my proposals for change. Like I said, I'm a change agent. In addition to all the changes mentioned above, I also suggested more focus groups with parents to better understand their needs. I suggested after-school programs, better reading programs, and more support for teachers in the classrooms. I also suggested a parent representative group for Latino and Native American families.

Of course, one of my focuses was suicide prevention. During my interview, I laid out ideas on how we could become more involved with suicide prevention. After the loss of the last student, I had done as much research as I could on the subject. I had talked with school psychologists, counselors, and even a social worker. From these meetings, it was obvious to me that we needed to do more training and give more support for our school staff in the area of prevention. But we would need help.

In the past, public schools had received grants to help promote drug prevention during the "War on Drugs," a prevention revolution against using illegal drugs. This funding was made possible by Nancy Reagan's "Just Say No" campaign, which focused attention on the issue.

In 1999, while the war on drugs continued, a new national crisis was coming to the forefront, a crisis we in Provo had been experiencing for more than ten years. The crisis was youth suicide! It was frightening and, for us, out of control. But the issue wasn't gaining enough attention yet for a "War on Youth Suicide."

During this time, few people recognized that Provo still had a problem with youth suicide. Just a few years before, *Money* magazine had named Provo as America's Most Livable City. But while there were many good things about Provo, no one talked about the loss of children. The school district had averaged one to two suicides a year for more than ten years.

After I finished my presentation, I could tell that my first interview with the committee was a flop, and I could see that change was not on the agenda. In fact, one of the members of the committee informed me that they were not looking for change. I was, however, invited for a second interview. While I was hopeful, it did not go well.

Nonetheless, the superintendent who was part of the second interview committee saw something different. He called me the night after the interview to inform me that I did not get the curriculum position, but he then invited me to his office the next morning.

I thought I was in trouble for all my suggestions. He shared with me that he loved my proposal and felt that it had merit. He also told me that he wanted me to be part of his leadership team at the district office. This was quite an honor, as I saw him as a true leader.

He had come from the outside and had been in our district for only a few years. I loved his style of leadership. He empowered others and believed that if you surround yourself with the best, they will help you shine. He did not get threatened. In fact, he thrived in putting his team out front and letting them have their share of the power and glory.

I thought, *I would love to work for this guy!* I asked the superintendent what position I would fill and he said, "I want you to be the student service director." I politely reminded him that he already had a district student service director and even some assistant directors.

He smiled and said, "I know. You'll be the new student service director."

I asked, "What will happen to the old one?"

Once again, he smiled and said, "You'll figure it out."

This job offer represented a tough decision for me. But eventually, my commitment to doing something about suicides in our schools helped me decide. Taking this position would give me the opportunity to make suicide prevention a priority at the district level. I could "rally the forces" to better support schools in crisis.

I accepted the offer and told him how grateful I was for the opportunity. It would become one of the most challenging assignments I had ever had. When you are at the school level, you tend to hate the district office. I was to find out why everyone hated the district and to experience why it was so difficult to make changes.

With this new job offer, I was now officially done with being a high school principal, but I had one more thing to do. When I met with the district leadership team, I asked to be in charge of interviewing for my replacement at the high school. At first, everyone had concerns, but then the superintendent said, "Let's let Greg be in charge of this. He knows the school, the kids, and the parents better than anyone else, and besides, who better to pick his replacement?"

Everyone smiled in approval because they knew I wanted my assistant principal, Judy, to take over. She was one of the finest people I had ever worked with. Behind the scenes, she made everything happen. I loved working with her and helped align the stars so she could take over as principal. She had worked hard as a teacher, counselor, and assistant principal. No one deserved the title of principal more than she did.

She had been one of the many talented people I had always surrounded myself with, and she always made me look good. These people were some of the finest educators in Utah. They cared about kids and worked hard to help students succeed. I was honored to consider them my fellow educators. They were also willing to buck the system to make it better. Many kids' lives were changed because of their commitment. I would miss working at the high school with such fine people.

As I made the move to the district, I brought my secretary, Donna, who had been with me for many years. She was sharp and could do anything. I called her my walking computer because she reminded me of a character from the old television series *MASH*. On the show, the colonel had a secretary who knew ahead of time what was going to happen and was thus nicknamed "Radar." Donna was my Radar and was always prepared before I even knew it. A few years later, I would bring my other secretary, Liz. She spoke fluent Spanish and was our connection to the Hispanic community.

SEEING ACADEMIC SUCCESS

While working at the district, I gained a wider perspective of our school system. Of the forty-one school districts in Utah, only three were city districts—Provo, Ogden, and Murray.

This made our life much easier with bussing, with community partnerships, and even with bonding for new schools. It also helped that Provo was in the middle of the state and most state and federal agencies were in our city. At the time, we were the seventh-largest school district in Utah, with twelve thousand students. Our urban school district was made up of thirteen elementary schools, three middle schools, and three high schools.

Provo was also home to Brigham Young University. This benefited us as a district because the college provided an exceptional support system with tons of college students wanting to volunteer and intern.

However, being a college town could also be a challenge because of the number of rentals in our community. We were a community of about ninety thousand. The trial was that we were struggling with having enough families. We had way too many rentals and way too many families coming and going.

Nevertheless, for the previous ten years, the Provo City School District was nationally recognized as one of the top academic districts in the country. Our graduates were headed to college in Utah and other universities across the country. Timpview High School, with its twenty-one hundred students, had one of the top programs in the state, and it had more of its kids going to Ivy League schools than almost any other school in the state.

Because of this national recognition, many educational institutions had looked to the Provo City School District as one of the finest models in academics. As a principal, I had numerous visits to my school from other districts and educators in Utah, as well as from other states.

While a principal, I received a phone call from a BYU professor, who shared that he had been at a national educational conference in California. A national speaker was talking about changes in education and the need for reform. When he opened it up for questions, someone from the audience asked for names of schools that were cutting-edge and making a difference.

The speaker mentioned schools in California, Texas, and Florida. He then talked about a smaller Utah high school that was creative and having great success—Independence High School. The BYU professor admitted he had no idea that such a successful school was in his backyard! I felt blessed to have been part of the success at Independence High School.

So there we were as a district, the envy of public academics in and out of Utah. And yet, we were also the school district that frightened and frustrated the mental health world. We were losing kids to suicide, and, as a system, we did not seem to care. I would learn later that it was not only Provo struggling, but that Utah as a state was losing kids to suicide.

Overcoming Challenges

After a few weeks of working at the district, I was honestly starting to wonder if I had made the right decision to go to the district office. It's one thing to go as the assistant superintendent with a job description and everything laid out for your daily routine. But in the world of academics, it's a whole different challenge when you are the new kid on the block and you happen to have the exact same title as someone who was still at the district office and had been there for years.

Then one word was added to my title: *senior*. I was the senior student service director, which meant that I was working above the existing student service director. In fairness to the individual I was now over, he had not been informed and had no idea what was going on until I "moved in." To say it was uncomfortable is an understatement. There I was, a change agent with the superintendent expecting me to "shake things up," and this poor guy thought I was sent to work under him.

Beside the director, the student service department was made up of five people: two secretaries, two former assistant principals, and a grant writer/researcher. They were all close after being together for years, and they were good at what they did.

I was the "outsider."

Not only were there already staff members and a director for student services, but there was no room in the "inn" for Donna and me. We showed up with our boxes, computers, and supplies, and there was no office, nor office furniture. When I spoke with the director of facilities, he told me that people were not happy with the decision by the superintendent. His decision had surprised everyone, especially the current student services director.

When I asked about my office, he replied, "You're the new student services director—you figure it out!" While the facility guy was cranky anyway, this took me completely by surprise. I outranked him with my title and status as a new cabinet member, but I was to find out that the title meant nothing.

I left the facility guy to go to the student services director's office. As soon as I walked in, I could tell they were angry. Even the two secretaries were rude to me. One turned her back to me when I asked a question and the other let me know that I would have to wait until the director was ready for me.

When I met with him, I could tell he was upset and frustrated, and I could not blame him. I was surprised that the superintendent had not met with him or warned him about my new position. Everyone had known about the new assistant superintendent, but no one except the personnel director had known about my new assignment.

When I asked about office space, I was told that the current offices were filled and that I would have to figure it out with facilities. When I replied that I had met with them and they directed me to him, he smiled and wished me luck.

My office was moved three times. My secretary and I had to move it by hand each time. Once we ended up out in the warehouse. Every time the forklift would move, our desks and chairs would rattle and things would get knocked down.

My one bright spot was the opportunity to work with Rod Crockett, one of my original mentors from when I was a young, inexperienced administrator. He was like a father to me and he helped mold me into the leader I was to become. He was a man without guile, and he was one of the best men Provo ever had. He believed in people and was willing to risk helping them be successful.

Another bright spot appeared when I was asked to serve as a cabinet member with the superintendent's team. We met weekly. There were five of us on the team and we pretty much ran the entire district under the leadership of the superintendent. I loved working and learning from this group of academic experts.

The negative was that when something came up that did not fit into curriculum, personnel, or finance, it was dumped into my lap. Soon I was closing schools, purchasing property, and negotiating with the city over concerns. Though sometimes the assignments didn't fit into my job description, they helped me become a better leader and would open doors in the future.

While my work at the district was slowly going better, the district was still losing one to two kids a year. Unfortunately, because of my many other responsibilities, suicide prevention had taken a back seat during my first year. But I would later realize that the move to the district office had helped me become a more rounded leader who better understood and appreciated mental illness, which greatly helped me on the path to suicide prevention.

Though my focus had to be on academics and the programs I oversaw, I was still pulled into the world of suicide.

In my first month at the district, I received a call from a coworker. She was in the emergency room with her son and asked if I could help. I ran over and met with her and her husband. Their seventeen-year-old son had attempted suicide for the second time in less than a year. The young man had been diagnosed three years earlier with severe depression.

As she shared her story, she told me that they had five children. This son, a middle child, was the only one in the entire family who had been diagnosed with a mental illness. She said that they had borrowed against their home, from their retirement, and from family members to try to save their child.

He had been in two residential treatment programs and a wilderness program, and then they'd gone back to meds. She told me that they were at their wits' end. Some nights, she just wished he would succeed and they could have their lives back. She then cried and said she was sorry, that she didn't mean it. She was just worn out.

I get it!

I'd been worn out by spending too many late nights in the emergency room with someone whose child had attempted or died by suicide.

These children weren't crazy or doing anything for attention. Those and similar statements are misconceptions that come to the minds of people who don't fully understand the challenges with mental illness. These children were crying out for help. They were in so much pain, and they just wanted that pain to end.

It broke my heart to see what these families were going through. There is no special pixie dust to make suicides magically disappear. I have seen both sides—the pain of the loss and the joy of the early intervention. I have learned that suicide is a complicated tragedy that shouldn't be written off by common misconceptions.

⊙ LIFESAVER ⊙
COMMON MISCONCEPTIONS
ABOUT SUICIDE

The act of suicide has existed through the ages, spanning many time periods and affecting many cultures. Ideas about suicide have evolved during this time, including many misconceptions. People who are not suicidal usually have a hard time understanding how someone could be suffering so much that he or she would attempt suicide. Thus, they perceive the misconceptions as truth.

Misconceptions[1] about suicide include the following:

"People who talk about suicide won't really do it."

Not true. The vast majority of those who attempt or are lost to suicide give warnings beforehand. Such warnings include statements like, "You'll be sorry when I'm dead," or "I can't see any way out." Do not ignore statements like this, even if they were said jokingly, because it can still indicate serious issues.

"Anyone who tries to kill himself/herself must be crazy."

Not true. Though there are those who are insane or psychotic, most suicidal people are deeply distressed or depressed (among other conditions). But just because someone is feeling extreme emotional pain does not mean that he or she has a mental illness or will attempt suicide.

"If a person is determined to kill himself/herself, nothing is going to stop them."

Not true. There are many resources to help suicidal individuals. They can be helped because, most of the time, they don't truly want to die. They just don't want to live with their pain anymore. Suicide is seen as a method to end this pain, but those individuals won't always see suicide as such.

"People who commit suicide are people who were unwilling to seek help."

Not true. Of those people who commit suicide, over half of them tried to get medical help during the six months before their suicide.

CALL TO ACTION

It is important to know that the above views are incorrect. This knowledge helps us begin to understand those who suffer and to be more compassionate toward them. Educate those around you who believe these misconceptions. Debunking these misconceptions is vital for effective suicide prevention.

NOTE

1. Adapted from information found at "Common Misconceptions about Suicide," La Frontera Arizona: Empact—Suicide Prevention Center, accessed January 26, 2018, http://lafrontera-empact.org/resources/common-misconceptions-about-suicide.

CHAPTER 7

Surrounded by Suicide

Working at the district office was a challenge for me. I was used to being the principal and being in charge. I was to learn rather quickly that I was part of a large bureaucracy and change would be difficult. I also started to understand why parents were so frustrated with the public educational system.

One challenge I faced had to do with a Utah law stating that any agency with an educational system in their organization had to be overseen by the local board of education. Because we were the second largest city in Utah and were located in the center of the state, we had numerous state and federal agencies in our backyard. Because we had the only state hospital in Utah, a large mental health agency, a detention center, an observation and assessment center, a "Youth in Custody" program, and numerous residential treatment programs for kids, I was responsible for more than twenty-five hundred students in a variety of state organizations.

Many of the programs I was assigned to had never had a district person over them. When I would show up to learn more about their program, they were nervous because no had ever stopped by before. It took time to convince them that I was on their side.

The first time I went to visit one of these state institutions, I had a hard time getting past the guards at the security doors. It was a little intimidating. When I finally got through to meet with the academic staff, they wanted to know who I was and what the heck I wanted. They informed me that in their many years there they had never been visited by someone from the district.

I was to face the same situation in many of the school programs I was assigned to visit. It would take me years to work with these individuals to develop trust and create change, but it was a rewarding challenge.

LOSING A TEACHER TO SUICIDE

Four months into my new assignment, I met with the superintendent to review my yearly goals. As he was reviewing my goals, he said, "Greg, suicide prevention is your number one goal?"

I replied that it was.

"So when will you have time to do the other things you're responsible for?"

I smiled and assured him that I would do everything that I was assigned to do.

He smiled back and said, "I know you will; that's why I recruited you. However, while I'm supportive of suicide prevention, please understand that I believe the local agencies should take care of those concerns while we focus on the classroom."

He then went on to tell me that suicide prevention should be moved down my priority list and that "if I had time, I could work on it." He tasked me with improving the academic programs in the facilities I was responsible for. He reminded me again that our mission was learning and that we needed to stick to it!

I accepted his counsel and assured him I would make sure we were successful in all my assignments and with all the programs and people I supervised. It was a huge undertaking, but I felt up to the challenge. I had a great staff who loved the opportunity to be of service to the programs.

Though I worked hard to prioritize my goals as the superintendent had counseled, I found myself still surrounded by suicide. My peers and most educators in our school district knew me as a compassionate leader who would do all that he could to help prevent suicides. Weekly, I would get someone stopping by my office to ask for help for a family member or friend dealing with depression or mental illness. I had secretaries, directors, teachers, and even custodians stop by to chat. The conversations always started with talk about families and vacations, but they invariably turned to a struggling family member. People were hurting.

At the time, suicide prevention could not be my top priority; however, I did give it as much time as I could. I was allowed to use a small grant to hire a person to help focus on suicide prevention. Her name was Cathy. She was a former teacher and a city PTA president, and she was concerned about the youth in our community. Behind the scenes, she was the one who made everything move forward with suicide prevention (education), intervention (reaching out for help), and postvention (support after a suicide), because I did not have the time.

On one occasion, I did have a chance to attend a conference back east that focused on working with mentally ill children. I got approval to attend because of my assignment with the state hospital. When I got to the conference, I found a break-out session on suicide postvention dealing with crisis intervention.

I wanted to improve our programs by learning as much as I could on how best to support schools and families. While I was at the conference, I received a call about a teacher who had died. The district crisis team had responded and provided support to everyone at the school.

We had told everyone that this teacher had died of a heart attack, because that's what the spouse told us. We then learned that he had taken his life by suicide. The last person he had visited with was a fellow teacher at the school. When word got out, it was chaos. I had to fly back immediately to help. It was a mess.

It can be difficult to admit that a family member has died by suicide. It goes along with the stigma of mental illness. As a society, we sometimes link mental illness with being crazy. People are afraid to let others know that a family member has died by suicide. The fear is that people will think their family member was crazy. In reality, we are usually dealing with someone who had struggled with a mental illness.

The other unfortunate issue is that we think we can protect the person who died by suicide by hiding the facts. But because of social media and other communication methods, the truth eventually gets out, and that can be hard on a family.

To help the family and community affected by a suicide, a good crisis team goes into a "crisis situation" with the intent of preventing another suicide and to have a return to normalcy as soon as possible for the school and community.

It took a week to calm things down and get help to the families who needed it. After returning from the conference, I immediately went to visit the school. I was walking down the hallway to see how everyone was doing. As I came around a corner, I could hear someone sobbing. It was the custodian. He was beside himself with grief. We sat and visited for over an hour. He knew the teacher well and liked him a lot. He shared that he would visit with this teacher often. They both had been at the school a long time and were close. The custodian knew the teacher was struggling, but he had no idea it was this bad.

Once again, we were reminded of the importance of training before a suicide and supporting after a suicide. The teacher had called a fellow staff member to visit before he took his life. I felt bad for the other staff member, because he was a really sharp guy. He, too, had no idea his fellow educator was going to kill himself.

I was finding out that suicide was everywhere and actually affected the adults in our community more than the youth. The highest rate of suicide was for ages forty-four to fifty-five. While our focus was on the youth, we would occasionally be dragged into an adult suicide situation, and it was heartbreaking.

LEARNING ABOUT MENTAL ILLNESS

As I visited my assigned state agency programs, I started to ask questions about mental illness. The more I learned about the subject, the more I learned about the families who struggle with the challenges that come with mental illness.

Going to the district office was the best thing I could have done to learn about mental illness from the ground up. These mental health experts introduced me to struggling families and students, and they showed me that there was a need for us to do more. It was obvious that educators were not aware of these daily challenges. The stigma is bad enough, and when you add ignorance, it becomes worse.

While at the district, I was able to take advantage of our local mental health agency. Utah's mental health services are divided into fourteen areas. Provo's local mental health agency is Wasatch Mental Health.

Because they were in our district, we were required to provide academic support. There I met amazing staff who cared about these kids. On one visit I was introduced to Doran Williams, one of the directors of the programs. He was supportive of my numerous questions, and he taught me a lot. He was also willing to challenge the way the district did things.

Doran helped me understand the challenges facing our children. He also helped me understand how difficult the school system is to maneuver for parents who have a mentally ill child. He once said to me, "Greg, have you ever tried to call a school during the day and speak to a live person?"

I laughed and said, "Sure, I do it every day."

He then said, "You do it as a district administrator. Try it as a local citizen."

I took him up on it and grabbed his phone and called one of the school numbers that parents are given. It rang and rang. After the tenth ring, the secretary answered. I asked to speak to the principal. She asked who was calling, and I made up a name. She replied, "Just a minute."

I waited for more than ten minutes before hanging up. He was right! I was used to calling on our district phones, where the secretaries could see the number and would always answer immediately. What I learned is that our school staff were overworked and undermanned.

Have you ever tried to call a school doing school hours? It is difficult for most people to even talk to a human being. While the secretaries would love to be able to answer the phone, they are dealing with hundreds of students, angry parents, sick children, and teachers who forgot their passcode for the copy machine.

As school systems, we expect them to answer their phones after the first ring with a smile and cheerful attitude. In most cases, school staff are not trained or equipped to work with mentally ill children or their families. Maneuvering through the system can be especially frustrating for a parent of a child who is struggling with mental illness.

That experience of calling the school opened my eyes to one of the many challenges that students with mental health were facing. Doran continued to open doors for me that I never realized existed in the world of mental illness. Through his efforts, I was introduced to Nedra, the volunteer coordinator with the National Alliance on Mental Illness (NAMI). I was then introduced to Dr. Ken Tuttle with the Intermountain Healthcare outreach program and Dr. Mark Payne and Dallas Earnshaw with the state hospital. They became my mentors in dealing with students struggling with mental illnesses.

The teacher was becoming the student. I was learning more about the challenges of mental illness, the treatment required, and the lack of services for families. It was an education that would help us build our program.

I also learned that there were support systems in our community that we never used. In a crisis, people think to use the emergency room, but there are other places that can help, including mental health agencies (Wasatch Mental Health for us), Family Support and Treatment Center, and NAMI. It gave me hope that many resources were willing and able to help with crises such as suicide.

CHANGING THE DISTRICT CRISIS TEAM

The district had a crisis team, but it was made up of school counselors who did not have a background in crisis interventions. They were good counselors, but most of their time was spent on scheduling, meeting with parents and students, and focusing on career placement and college applications.

When I first started my career in education, our school counselors were master's-level individuals in either education or social work. They had more experience in understanding mental illness and systems theory. In fairness, they also had more time to work with kids one-on-one. Over time, these assignments changed, and the funding stream changed so that it came from the state vocational funds.

On the one hand, this makes sense because counselors help students look at options for careers after high school. The concern was that with this new funding stream, we saw a new type of student coming out of the college programs. They had more and more training in careers, but less and less training in working with troubled kids.

I had an experience with this change in counselors while I was a principal. After a suicide, I had a counselor who was struggling in her office. We visited, and I asked her how many classes she had taken in college about mental illness or suicide. She smiled and said that she remembered one class presentation on suicide. She admitted she was not prepared for these types of challenges.

Her lack of preparation was not her fault; she was a superb counselor who cared about kids and was respected by the students. But she did not have the skill set. Later on, I visited with a professor at one of our universities, and she informed me that they had stopped their school counseling program because the state was putting so much emphasis on career counseling.

One time a principal from a large high school that had four suicides in two years shared with me that after her first suicide, she went into the counseling center and asked the counselors what they should do. The experienced, knowledgeable counselors replied they had no idea what to do. She then told me that these counselors were some of the finest, most talented educators she had ever worked with. The challenge was that they did not have any training in working with mental illness or in crisis situations.

With these experiences in mind as I worked with all the state agencies, I was soon convinced that we needed to change the district crisis team to include those who knew how to handle suicide situations. I had seen firsthand the challenges within our system, and I had learned the training and understanding needed in a crisis situation. I also realized that we needed to provide more in-depth training to our counselors so they knew what to do and how best to respond.

I met with the school counselor, who was over the district crisis team. He was a good counselor and was respected throughout the district. The challenge was that our system needed to change. When I shared what I was learning about mental illness and the importance of having experts help us, he let me know in no uncertain terms that he was in charge of the crisis team and that it had worked well for the last ten years and that it would for the next ten years!

Later that day, I was in a meeting with the assistant superintendent. She and I had applied for the same position, and she'd gotten it. To be honest, I was glad she had. She was good at what she did, and I liked and respected her. I enjoyed visiting her and sharing frustrations and working out problems.

When I shared with her what I was working on, she asked, "Why don't you fix it?"

I asked, "What do you mean?"

She then replied, "Well, you're over that area, and it's your responsibility. If you feel we need to do something different and it's better for students, then change it."

Listening to her, I felt empowered. She was right. I was the administrator over that area, and I could change it. I thanked her and started putting together a plan to address it with the lead counselor and his supervisor.

After working on a proposal for change, I met with the lead counselor and shared my vision. While he was respectful, he reminded me that he was in charge, he didn't report to me, and changing the crisis team wasn't my call.

I started to get upset, but then I remembered my past secretary's challenge to have more quiet dignity and to respect the other person's opinion. So I listened and shared my thoughts and concerns and then informed him we would need to change. Despite my quiet dignity, the meeting did not end well.

I headed back to my office, and within ten minutes I had a call from the lead counselor's supervisor, who was quite upset. He came to meet with me, and we discussed his concerns for the next thirty minutes. He reminded me that he was in charge of the district crisis team.

When I tried to explain that all I wanted to do was to add volunteer experts from the local mental health agency, he exploded and said, "Public educators know what's best for kids. Please mind your own business and stay out of things you do not understand. We do not need help from outsiders, nor do we want it! Besides, you have only been here in the district office for less than six months. Quit trying to change everything!"

Change is difficult.

✪ LIFESAVER ✪
THE STIGMA WITH MENTAL ILLNESS

A stigma is "a sign of disgrace or discredit, which sets a person apart from others."[1]

There is certainly a stigma with mental illness.

When I was a principal, I was asked to sit in on an Individualized Education Program (IEP) meeting with my special education director and a mother who was a prominent citizen. The mother's son was three years behind in math, but she had refused any services and was upset about the situation.

The parent meeting I sat in on was set up because the student had failed his first semester math class as a junior, and the teacher was frustrated with the student and the mother.

During the parent meeting, I could see that the mother was not going to allow her son to receive special education services. I asked her why.

She replied, "I don't believe my son is stupid, and I don't want him put with those stupid kids."

I tried to help her understand that her son was failing his class and it was obvious that he needed additional help. She again refused help and demanded that he be placed back into his regular mainstream math class with no special education services.

At the end of the meeting, my special education director got up to leave and I asked if she was okay. She replied, "Unfortunately, there's a lot of stigma with special education."

These kids are not stupid; they just need more time, more attention, and a little boost.

We ended up putting the son back into his mainstream math class, and he failed. And to be honest, I felt like we had failed.

With the stigma, mental illness is seen as a sign of weakness. Those with mental illness are sometimes misdiagnosed because their symptoms are seen as behaviors that they will grow out of or just need to try harder to overcome.[2] Others often feel embarrassed for those with mental illness, and those with mental illness feel shame even though their mental illness is not in their control.[3] The stigma causes the shame, which makes people reluctant to get help or share that they are struggling.

This shame and avoidance of help can often lead to suicide. It is important to note that while the great majority of those with mental illness do not attempt suicide, about 90 percent of people who die from suicide suffered from a diagnosable mental illness.[4]

While I spent seven years supervising the state hospital educational program, I saw firsthand the challenges with mental illness. I saw how the stigma affected those who were suffering. It was always "those kids" who were mentally ill. It is obvious that the stigma was alive and well in our schools and in our communities. People with a mental illness are not crazy and cannot "get over" their mental illness.

CALL TO ACTION

Instead of feeding it, there are things we can do to stop the mental illness stigma, whether we are the ones with mental illness or not.

- ✿ Educate yourself and others.
- ✿ Encourage equality between physical and mental illness.
- ✿ Show compassion for those with mental illness.
- ✿ Choose empowerment over shame.
- ✿ Be honest about treatment.
- ✿ Let the media know when they're being stigmatizing.
- ✿ Don't harbor self-stigma.[5]
- ✿ [Be] open to conversations about mental health.
- ✿ [Be] respectful with language.
  - » Use person-first language. . . . A person *experiences* bipolar disorder—he's not bipolar. . . .

> » Be cautious when talking about suicide. . . . A person is "lost to suicide" or "died by suicide" rather than "committed suicide." . . .
> » Challenge misconceptions.
> » Don't use mental health conditions as adjectives.
> » Don't refer to someone as "crazy," "psychotic," or "insane."
> » Don't use the term "others" or "abnormal."

⟳ [Be] understanding of what you might not understand.
⟳ [Be] supportive of other people's struggle and recovery.
⟳ [Be] active in spreading mental health awareness.[6]

Many people suffer from mental illness. In any given year, "about one in five adults suffer from a diagnosable mental illness (disorder)."[7] We need to work together to stop the stigma that causes so much shame. I once heard a church leader say that struggling with a mental illness should be no more embarrassing than someone struggling with a broken arm or a sprained ankle. I love that tender mercy in helping us all better understand mental illness.

NOTES

1. Peter Byrne, "Stigma of Mental Illness and Ways of Diminishing It," *Advances in Psychiatric Treatment* 6, no. 1 (January 2000): 65, http://apt.rcpsych.org/content/6/1/65.
2. Laura Greenstein writing for NAMI, "9 Ways to Fight Mental Health Stigma," National Alliance on Mental Illness (NAMI), posted Oct. 11, 2017, https://www.nami.org/Blogs/NAMI-Blog/October-2017/9-Ways-to-Fight-Mental-Health-Stigma.
3. Greenstein writing for NAMI, "9 Ways to Fight Mental Health Stigma."
4. "Fact Sheets: Facts about Mental Illness and Suicide," *Mental Health Reporting*, School of Social Work University of Washington, http://depts.washington.edu/mhreport/facts_suicide.php.
5. Adapted from information found at Laura Greenstein writing for NAMI, "9 Ways to Fight Mental Health Stigma."
6. Adapted from information found at Laura Greenstein writing for NAMI, "How You Can Stop Mental Illness Stigma," National Alliance on Mental Illness (NAMI), posted May 1, 2017, https://www.nami.org/Blogs/NAMI-Blog/May-2017/How-You-Can-Stop-Mental-Illness-Stigma.
7. "Mental Illness and Suicide," Suicide Awareness Voices of Education (SAVE), accessed January 26, 2018, https://save.org/about-suicide/mental-illness-and-suicide.

CHAPTER 8

Suicide Prevention Is a Community-Wide Effort

About a week after being shot down for trying to change the district crisis team, another student attempted suicide. I heard about it from one of the folks I met out on my assignment at the local hospital. The hospital had a residential treatment program, and because that included an academic program, we provided teachers and support. As I was visiting, I met some of the therapists. I also met the supervisor, Dr. Ken Tuttle, who was the director of psychiatry care.

He was one of the kindest and most caring individuals I have ever met. He is also one of the most brilliant. I am sure I drove him crazy with all my questions, but he took the time to patiently answer them and help me understand. Within a short time, we became close friends. He was my mental health mentor.

Because of these relationships with people at the hospital, I would learn firsthand the number of kids who were attempting suicide and had been hospitalized. The number of kids in the program was staggering. The number was so great that within a short period of time, other psychiatric hospitals were coming to our community. The frightening part was that, in many situations, the district was not even aware that the kids had attempted.

Before long, I knew I had to get back into the business of suicide prevention or, as my new mentors had trained me, into the world of suicide prevention, intervention, and postvention. I decided to take the plunge, and I reached out to the many mental health experts I had met for help.

BUILDING A COMMUNITY TASK FORCE

Looking back, I realize I was lucky to be in this unique position at the district. It truly was a godsend, because it put me in the right place to again help with suicide prevention.

For many years, I served on the local hospital's Community Outreach Council. As I shared my concerns about suicide, they would encourage me to find ways to help the struggling kids in our system. Kye was the hospital guru, and after one of our monthly meetings, she pulled me aside and asked, "What are you going to do about it?" As we visited, I felt encouraged by her and others to do something about suicide prevention.

I started recruiting help by reaching out to the community and inviting a group of individuals to come to a lunch to talk about suicide. Just before the meeting started, my secretary, Donna, poked her head into my office and asked how many people I had invited. I told her, "Twelve or thirteen. Why?" She replied that there were close to thirty people in the room. I was skeptical. But then I heard noises and voices. I ran out to see what all the commotion was, and when I walked into the meeting room, to my surprise, it was full.

The room was packed with community leaders, agency directors, clergy members, and representatives from throughout the community. I asked them why they were all there. I will never forget the response from Tom, who was the Boy Scout council director of one of the largest councils in the country, with some fifty thousand scouts. He said, "Greg, these are our kids too!" It was at that moment that I knew this was going to be a community-wide effort, and I was grateful for their support.

Together, we created a community task force and named our group the Utah County Hope Task Force. In 1999, we started meeting monthly. We spent that first year learning about suicide from the experts. At our monthly meetings, we brought in mental health experts to partner with and educate us. These professional folks (therapists, psychologists, law enforcement, etc.) would become our community crisis team. The mental health folks would come to our meetings and share the latest research. I saw early on that not only were educators behind in the learning process, but so were many other agencies.

We spent hours and hours researching, visiting with families who lost children, and learning all that we could about mental illness, depression, and youth suicide. Once word got out that we were establishing a community-wide task force, it was amazing to see the people who wanted to be a part of it.

Everything we did and accomplished was because of their skills and the acknowledgment that our community was in crisis.

The time spent on the task force and in monthly meetings was nothing like your average meetings, where everyone agreed on everything. We debated, disagreed, and spent hours hashing out ideas and proposals. While it could be a challenge, I gained much knowledge from my comrades.

This was a process.

Up to that point, there had been little national attention on suicide prevention. But that was about to change. During a conference in Reno, Nevada, Surgeon General David Satcher issued his "Call to Action to Prevent Suicide," which emphasized suicide as a serious public health problem, asked for attention to be directed at the problem, and demanded action.[1]

It was refreshing to have someone "high up" recognize the problem of suicide. Unfortunately, sometimes it takes a while to get the ball rolling, even with a national call to action like that. While the "call to action" went out across the country, we felt that we were fighting it alone in Utah. Luckily, we had critical resources that helped us fight and learn more about suicide and how to prevent it.

Our task force collaborated with and learned from our state's best and brightest minds in the mental health arena. Provo had the only state hospital, which meant we had access to some of the most talented psychiatrists, psychologists, and social workers—people who dealt with the most serious mentally ill patients. These experts shared their expertise and experiences with us, and we learned a lot from them.

We learned that between 1981 and 1999, suicide rates for children ages ten to fourteen increased by 50 percent.

We learned that youth suicide was one of the major causes of death in our state; even more youths were lost to suicide than to accidents or diseases. Adults ages forty-five to fifty had one of the highest rates. We learned that in many cases, mental illness began between the ages of ten and fourteen and that if we could identify young people who were struggling, we had a good chance of preventing suicide.

We learned that 1 to 5 percent of all youth suicides was a copycat, and with the loss of more young people, this could turn into a contagion if we did not intervene. We also learned that about 20 percent of our young people who died by suicide left notes.

I learned that suicide is individualized and complex. Sometimes there isn't a way to pinpoint an exact reason for the suicide. What causes one person to give up in life could be nothing more than an irksome situation for another person, depending on the situation and mental health of the individuals.

I learned so much, and I could hardly believe that my second year at the district office had already ended. I made a lot of site visits, met new people in the academic programs, and once again was pulled into the world of suicide prevention. I had to be careful to not let this overtake my responsibilities at the district office. I was constantly reminded that "suicide was my interest, not the district's!" While it could not be my top priority, it was still a passion that was growing inside me.

☉ LIFESAVER ☉
What to Say and
What Not to Say

Through many years of working with youth and through working on the community task force, I found that in many cases people (including myself at first) don't know what to do or say in a suicide situation. Knowing what to say and what not to say is one of the basic first steps in suicide prevention.

Call to Action

If someone approaches you saying they are thinking of suicide or are otherwise struggling, the most important things you can do include the following:

1. Give them your total attention.
2. Put your phone away.
3. Move to a private setting, if you are not already in one.
4. Listen, listen, and listen to what they are saying.
5. Watch your body language; how you act is as important as what you say.
6. Be sympathetic, non-judgmental, patient, calm, and accepting.
7. Offer hope.
8. Take the person seriously.[2]

When you are with that person, be present in mind, body, and spirit. People can tell very quickly whether or not you are sincere, and that will dictate if they close off to you or open up even more and accept help.

Beside knowing what to do, you may also need help knowing what to say. Effective phrases that use the "I" message include the following:

1. "I noticed you seemed to be struggling today. Is everything okay?"
2. "I am worried about you."
3. "How can I help?"
4. "I am here for you."
5. "I may not understand what you are going through, but I am here to listen and to help."
6. "What can I do to help?"

While there are many helpful things you can say or do as you converse with someone who is struggling, there are also several important things to NOT do or say.

Working with many youths who struggle with depression and even suicide, I have heard them say that comments such as the following "turned them off" when people thought they were helping:

1. "It's not that bad."
2. "You will get over this and find someone else."
3. "Just suck it up."
4. "The sun will rise, and everything will be fine."
5. "You're not suicidal, are you?" (Tone probably played a factor here.)
6. "I promise you will grow out of this."

Some things to NOT do include the following:

1. Argue with the suicidal person.
2. Act shocked.
3. Promise confidentiality.
4. Offer ways to fix their problems.
5. Blame yourself.[3]

By following (or not following) the suggestions in these lists, you can make a discussion about suicide a positive experience and guide someone to get the help he or she needs.

NOTES

1. U.S. Public Health Service, *The Surgeon General's Call to Action to Prevent Suicide* (Washington, DC: 1999).
2. "Suicide Prevention: How to Help Someone Who Is Suicidal and Save a Life," HelpGuide.org, accessed January 26, 2018, https://www.helpguide.org/articles/suicide-prevention/suicide-prevention.htm.
3. Ibid.

CHAPTER 9

The Courage to Change

Our task force continued to work toward suicide prevention, and our mantra became our guiding light: "While it takes an entire village to raise a child, we believe it takes an entire community to save one." Being an educator, I knew firsthand the value of having everyone in my class understand basics about what I was teaching and wanting them to know. The same held true for the community task force.

The more we met as a community task force, the more we wanted to find a way to help educate anybody and everybody in our community. We wanted everyone to understand the basics of suicide prevention. From my days working at Independence High School, I had learned the importance of everybody (even the custodian and lunch lady) knowing what to do in suicide situations. The staff there would see and hear things from students that no one else would, including their families. I saw firsthand the importance of having everyone trained—suicide prevention needed "all hands on deck."

Over the next six months at the district, I convinced the superintendent to allow me to train all our employees every three years. To this day, every bus driver, secretary, custodian, lunch lady, teacher, and administrator in Provo City School District gets trained on suicide prevention every three years. As of 2017, we have been doing this for over fifteen years.

These trainings would be the single most important thing we would do as a district to help prevent suicides.

One of the experiences that helped solidify the importance of training was an experience by one of our bus drivers. About six months after we had trained the bus drivers to recognize the warning signs of suicide, one of our bus drivers was taking home the after-school kids from a middle school. As he was unloading the last group, he heard one of the students make a comment to a friend about not wanting to live anymore. It was an offhand comment, and the driver wasn't sure what he heard.

On the way back to the bus compound, he thought about it again and again. When he arrived at the compound, he decided to call the school and share what he had overheard. The school called me, and because it was a Friday night and the counselors were gone, I decided to handle it. As I was preparing to check up on the student, I ran into the school psychologist. He said he knew the student and would love to go.

It was a Friday night with football in session, so I dropped by the high school field and asked one of the school resource officers (SROs) to help us. He was one of my favorites and would do anything and everything to prevent children from hurting themselves.

We drove to southwest Provo to a large apartment complex. The SRO was waiting for us. We went to the door, and after a discussion, the SRO was invited in. The school psychologist and I waited outside. When the SRO came out, he informed us that the young man had a plan to kill himself that very night and had the stuff to do it.

This seventh grader's mom was in prison and his father had passed away. He was living with his grandma and grandpa. Unfortunately, his grandpa was in the hospital with cancer, and they did not think he was going to make it. This young man had given up hope and felt like he was becoming a burden to his family.

If it were not for the alert bus driver, we may have lost another child.

HELPING THE DISTRICT
WITH A SUICIDE

One of the early suicides that would help unite us as a community crisis team was a suicide by a ninth grader. He was a great kid who fell into the wrong crowd. He attended a high school on the east side of town. This school, like all the others, had great kids and great staff members. Unfortunately, it was also like all the other secondary schools in that it had many kids who were struggling.

The young man and some of his peers got caught breaking school rules. The SRO called the young man's home and informed his mom that he was being suspended. She told her son to walk home, because he lived close to the school. When he got home, his mom told him to go to his room and wait for his father to get home. My wife would have said the same thing.

So he went to his room, and within a short time, the mother heard a noise downstairs. He had taken his life by suicide using the gun under his bed (it was a gun that he hunted with). He was a popular baseball player and was loved by his peers, and his parents were well respected in the community. It was a huge loss. Once again, we were dealing with the death of one of our students.

I got the call from the police department informing me of the death, and they asked if I could meet the officer there at the house. By the time I got there, the driveway was filled with police cars, ambulances, and neighbors. As I stepped out of my car, I could see the fear in everyone's eyes.

As soon as I was done talking with the officer, I drove immediately to the young man's school and could see that the counselors were visibly shook up. In fact, most of the counselors were struggling because they knew the student well and had worked with him. Most of the school staff were also struggling, including the administration. When I asked the counselors if they needed any additional help, the lead school counselor replied, "Yes, please help us."

I could tell this was going to be a difficult one to deal with. We reached out for help from a few community members. It went well. In fact, the lead school counselor told me afterward that he was grateful for the expertise shared by one of the therapists.

The district crisis team members had been notified and they showed up to help. But it was the skill set of the professional therapists from Wasatch Mental Health and Intermountain Healthcare, as well as members of the Family Support and Treatment Center, who made the difference. They were the example to the rest of the district crisis team.

You would think that by this point our district crisis team would have had enough experience to deal with any and every crisis. It's not that we did not have the skill set, but death was unique and challenging. We learned not to take things for granted as we responded to each crisis and each suicide. Each suicide attempt or death happened around each individual and their exclusive situation.

It's also difficult when you deal with one suicide a year or every two years, as some of the team members had.

That night at the school, I got to see and experience the emotions on both sides. On the one hand, the staff were relieved by the presence of the professionals, but on the other hand, the district crisis team was put out by having the professionals there. The school folks thanked me at the end of the day.

Unfortunately, our district crisis team leader did not feel the same way that I did about inviting the experts to be part of our team. In fact, he let it be known that I was "out of my league" in working with families in crisis. He tried his best to chew me out and intimidate me. When he was done yelling at me, he stormed out. I hadn't had a chance to say much; sometimes the less said, the better.

My secretary, Donna, stuck her head in the doorway and asked if I was okay. I gave a weak smile and replied that I was fine. But I wasn't fine. I was getting tired of working in a broken system. I was also starting to get frustrated with individuals who believed the system existed only for them. Sometimes it felt like we forgot that we were public servants.

And we were still losing kids. I was tired of feeling like we as a school system were afraid to do things differently. I knew that we needed help from the experts. I also knew that change at the top can be difficult to obtain.

The next day, my secretary walked in and told me the superintendent was waiting for me. When I walked into his office, he asked me to review what happened with the last suicide. When I was finishing up, I looked at him and asked, "I sort of feel like this was not as much a follow-up to the crisis but more of a chance to see what really happened. Am I right?"

He smiled and replied, "Actually, there have been some concerns brought to my attention. I wanted to hear your side of the story."

I was not sure what to say, so I then asked, "So what do you think?"

He replied, "I'm not sure at this time; however, it's obvious that you are trying to help those schools that are in crisis and to support families. I'm not sure I can find fault with that. Although it appears that you've offended some folks that have been doing things the same way for many years. However, maybe it's time to shake things up."

I did like this superintendent! I found, however, that it would take more suicides to change the norm in our district.

UNITING WITH THE
DISTRICT CRISIS TEAM

Unfortunately, it took a suicide by another ninth grader to change the way the district did business with the community crisis team. One of our high school freshmen, who was well liked and appeared to be successful in life, came to school one day and at lunchtime took his watch off and gave it to his best friend. He then told his friend, "My family will be better off without me. I'm going to kill myself."

He went on to share with three or four other students that he was contemplating taking his life or that he was wanting to die, and not one of those young people told an adult, not even their parents. The next day, this amazing young person took his life. It was devastating.

The day of the suicide, I got the call from the police department. I went to the school to meet with the principal and the counselors to see what I could do to help. This happened to be the school where the director of the district crisis team was a counselor. They were polite but assured me that they had it under control and for me "to not worry about it."

Later that night, this high school was playing their district rival in football. My son was on the team, so my wife and I went to the game and sat in the bleachers. By the time I got out of my car, many spectators were asking me about the suicide. This kid was popular. I assured them that it was under control. I remember turning to my wife and saying, "At least, I hope it's under control."

About halfway through the first quarter, one of the assistant principals came looking for me. He asked if I could come to the principal's office right away. In my gut, I knew we were in trouble. When I got to the front of the school, there were probably 150 kids there. They were crying, screaming, punching the walls, and just holding each other, sobbing.

I walked into the school and saw that not only were the kids struggling but so were the adults. The counselors were beside themselves. They were all sobbing and struggling with the news of the suicide. I asked the principal what I could do and he said, "Greg, please help us."

I jumped on the phone and had Cathy call all our crisis team members from the community. About ten minutes later, therapists from the Family Support and Treatment Center showed up. Then the crisis team from the hospital arrived.

Wasatch Mental Health folks also came to help. Before long, we had twenty community crisis team folks there working with the kids and the adults. These folks were willing to help, and it made the difference.

We were at the school until one a.m. As we were wrapping up, one of the community folks suggested we have a "crisis team debriefing" with everyone, including the school counselors and administration. We were all tired physically, and even more emotionally.

Despite our exhaustion, we gathered everyone for the debriefing. We went around the circle of twenty-plus people and took turns sharing our thoughts, experiences, and anything we were struggling with. One of the top therapists I admired and respected shared her experiences with some of the kids. She mentioned names of kids she was worried about and informed the counselors they needed to follow up with the parents of those kids.

Then she broke down and started to cry. She expressed how tough this was and how emotionally draining it can be. Everyone cried. It was healthy for all of us to share the experience. I felt a kindred spirit to these folks because of the emotional battle we had just been through.

The funeral was difficult and it was one that taught us the importance of focusing more on postvention than we had in the past.

At the funeral, American flags were strung out along the road to the church, and Boy Scouts attended in uniform, because the young man had just attained the rank of Eagle Scout. The church was filled with flowers. It looked like a dignitary's funeral. The church was packed; hundreds of people attended. The focus was on how wonderful the young man was and what a wonderful life he lived. No one at the pulpit mentioned the word *suicide*.

Unfortunately, we would have two copycat attempts within a week. It was another lesson for the community about the importance of not glamorizing the incident. Postvention is a critical part of suicide prevention.

The next Monday I had a visit from the counselor of the district crisis team and the homeroom counselor of the school we had helped. In tears, he apologized and admitted he had been wrong. He asked for help and wondered if I would be willing to take over the district crisis team. It was emotional and yet the right thing that needed to happen. While I was now in charge of the crisis team, it would take years to convince everyone that collaboration with the experts outside the school district was crucial to our success.

In our next community task force meeting, I invited our district crisis team. The folks from the district were appreciative and grateful for the help. It was what needed to happen and a blessing for all of us as a community.

The lead counselor shared with the group that one of the things he appreciated most was the folks from the Family and Treatment Support Center. They had sent three therapists to help with the crisis. They had also met with a parent and made an appointment for their daughter. Afterward, the parent had visited with the school counselor and told him how grateful she was for the additional help.

We also learned a lot from the death of that ninth grader. From that experience, and later from others, we learned the importance of involving peers. The student had told his friends what he was planning to do, but no adults were ever made aware. I felt the need to do more with kids helping each other.

The high school principal met with the superintendent and shared what had happened and how grateful he was for the help and support from the community. He also told him that it would have been a nightmare for his school had it not been for everything that was done to help.

In our weekly cabinet meeting after that suicide, the superintendent shared the message from the principal. He turned to me and asked searching questions about the community partners. When he finished, he said, "I guess this is a good thing. I support you working on it."

That was it! I had the green flag to move ahead with suicide prevention from a district level and with support from the brightest mental health experts in the state. It would make the difference for our community.

The second year of my working at the district, the community task force and district crisis team focused on training and meeting every month. I was able to meet with school counselors, psychologists, and soon-to-be-hired social workers on a regular basis. We were lucky to have talented individuals in the helping business. They too were concerned about the number of suicides. We were also lucky to have the partnership with the local hospital, Intermountain Healthcare. We would work together as a team to help families in crisis.

Our district crisis team started to track information about students and suicide. We asked every counselor to track every student who was referred for help because of a mental health concern. We knew we were losing kids but didn't understand why. I wanted to see what the data told us. We would become one of the first school districts in the country that had data (over a fifteen-year period) of every student who threatened, attempted, or took their life by suicide.

Without realizing it, I had also developed the baseline for suicide information for the school district. Before our district crisis team, nobody was keeping track of suicide threats, attempts, or losses at the district level. The lack of tracking came back to haunt us because there were many suicide-related situations that we were not even aware of until we saw it in writing. However, tracking also helped us, because we could use the information to show the impact of suicide, the challenges with suicide prevention, and the need to deal with suicide as a district and as a community.

After one of our community meetings, I was back in the office thinking about what we had been discussing. There were many opinions and great ideas. Somehow, I just needed to put it together so it could make sense. I called Cathy into my office and I went to the whiteboard. On the side panel, I had white paper. With a marker, I laid out what was to become our "Circles4Hope" model.

I drew three circles and laid out the three areas. We first had to have the community on board and supporting suicide prevention. Then we needed mental health experts on board, and, finally, we needed schools' cooperation and help. The middle, where all the circles overlapped, became the focus of suicide prevention, intervention, and postvention.

Cathy would come back with a much better chart and more balanced interconnecting circles, but it was a start.

As our Circles4Hope model developed, we could truly see how involving an entire community was crucial to saving youth from suicide.

☺ LIFESAVER ☺
CRISIS LINE

One of our mental health experts once shared with me that connection is the key to preventing suicide. He went on to say that out of a hundred people struggling, only two or three ever need to go to the emergency room. What almost everyone needs is someone who cares and is willing to listen.

Our crisis team is full of caring people who are willing to listen, and it has helped and continues to help many struggling students. But if there is no crisis team in your community or you don't know who to contact when a crisis comes up, there are crisis lines that are always there to help.

Crisis lines are important resources for those struggling and for those trying to help someone who is struggling. I use the crisis line when I am working with an individual and am not sure what to do next. The professionals on the line have been responsive to sharing information about community resources.

Here are some useful resources to know if you or someone you know is in a crisis situation.

Local Crisis Line

Most communities have a local crisis line. Please pull out your phone and add your local crisis line number to your list of contacts. The crisis line in my community is sponsored by Wasatch Mental Health, the local mental health agency. They have a twenty-four-hour line manned by trained therapists. I use them all the time.

National Crisis Line

If you do not have access to a local crisis line, the National Suicide Prevention Lifeline is 1-800-273-TALK (8255). They are available 24/7 and every call is free and confidential. You can even chat online at suicidepreventionlifeline.org.

Crisis Text Line

Another resource is the Crisis Text Line (741741). This national resource could be particularly valuable for students, because some students would prefer to text than talk with someone when they are struggling emotionally. This line doesn't just help youth who are suicidal; they are willing to help with any crisis. To learn more about how the Crisis Text Line works, visit crisistextline.org.

Utah Crisis App

For people in Utah, there is an app called SafeUT, which I use all the time. This app is a crisis text and tip line that allows users to text, chat, or call licensed clinicians. It is confidential, available 24/7, and free to download and use. If you are in Utah, I encourage you to download it on your child's phone and show him or her how to use it. It is a valuable resource.

The Trevor Project

The Trevor Project provides crisis intervention and suicide prevention services for lesbian, gay, bisexual, transgender, and questioning (LGBTQ) youth. These services include a twenty-four-hour lifeline (866-488-7386), online chat, texting service (text "Trevor" to 1-202-304-1200), and a social media "safe place" (https://www.trevorspace.org).

CALL TO ACTION

Please take out your phone and add these phone numbers to your contacts. In many situations, talking to and being willing to listen to someone who is depressed can be the first step to helping him or her. Many of the students I have worked with shared with me that they felt lonely and that no one would listen to them. Talking with a trained professional crisis response member can help reduce stress levels.

Do not be afraid to reach out for help when you are in a crisis situation with someone who is threatening to hurt themselves or someone else, or if you are the person who is struggling. Call and ask questions or get advice. In an emergency, call 911.

PART 3

The Community:
If Not Us,
Then Who?

CHAPTER 10

The Battle against Suicide

The more we learned from our community experts as they trained the community task force and the district crisis team, the more we knew we needed to share this valuable information with other educators. We had amazing support throughout the community. Beside giving presentations and holding training, the community crisis team decided to hold a conference every year for educators.

We partnered with Professor Melissa Heath on an annual suicide prevention conference for educators, to be held on campus at Brigham Young University. We brought in experts to teach and train others about suicide prevention, intervention, and postvention.

It was a hit. Over time, I was able to get permission for all the Provo school counselors, psychologists, and social workers to attend. Over the years, we have even had administrators participate. These conferences helped us to identify not only the experts in our community but also the experts in our state. Within a few years, our suicide prevention conference became one of the top conferences for educators in Utah. It has been a wonderful success.

GAINING SUICIDE PREVENTION SUPPORT

While we continued training, the Utah Department of Health had heard what we were doing and invited us to be part of a statewide task force on suicide prevention. It was the first time we had a state agency step up to help us fight the war against youth suicide.

The taskforce committee was chaired by Trish Keller. She worked for the Utah Department of Health and was interested in suicide prevention. There were about a dozen people invited to be on the committee, including Dr. Doug

Gray. It was the second time I had the chance to work with him. Doug was considered one of Utah's experts on youth suicide prevention.

We had worked together a few years earlier when I was first getting into youth suicide prevention. He and I had been asked to help a high school up north after a suicide. I was impressed with his skill set and calm demeanor. He was easy to get along with. At the time I met him, he had just finished a longitudinal study on youth suicide in Utah.[1]

Doug's research was fascinating, and we were using many of the things he had learned through his research in our community program. For example, in his six-year study, he found that 40 percent of the youth who died by suicide had been involved with juvenile court. Because of this information, we were working closely with our juvenile court to monitor the youth sent there to see if they were at risk for depression or suicide.

Doug became my mentor and the person I would go to most when I was trying to figure things out. We met monthly for breakfast for many years.

Not long after this committee was formed, the United States Surgeon General put out a call to invite two people from every state to share what they were doing to prevent suicide, the challenges the state was facing, and, most important, what we thought the feds could do to help us. The feds knew there was a problem with suicide and wanted to know more from the states.

As a member of this committee, I had the chance to meet and work with other amazing people. Cal Cazier was one of those folks. He was an employee at the Utah Department of Health and an adjunct professor at Brigham Young University.

Cal and I were invited to represent Utah. It was quite an honor. Because of budget restraints, Cal and I shared a room at a hotel in DC, where the collaboration was held. We went out to dinner the night before the meeting and discussed what we were going to "testify" on. Being a state employee, Cal was focusing on the state as a whole, and I, of course, was focusing on kids.

At the time, I knew Cal had Tourette syndrome. He was by far one of the brightest individuals I had ever met. He inspired folks because he did not let his disability get in the way. His symptoms included involuntary and repetitive movements of his jaw and mouth. I found out later it also involved other symptoms.

Back in the hotel room after dinner, I mentioned to Cal that I was scared to present the next day. He just smiled and assured me that I would do fine. He then encouraged me to review my presentation that night so I would be ready in the morning, because we had to catch a six thirty a.m. bus.

I stayed up until about eleven p.m. reviewing and reviewing what I was going to say. Each presenter had been allotted seventeen minutes to make our mark, so I wanted to be ready. I read my scriptures and said my prayers and was off to sleep.

Around two thirty in the morning, I heard a loud yell. I sat up and saw Cal standing on his bed in his pajamas, yelling at the top of his lungs. He was screaming scary things. I sat frozen in my bed. I did not know what to do. Do I say something? If I did, would he turn on me?

After a good five minutes, he stopped, climbed back under his sheets, and was sound asleep in a second. To be honest, I had stopped breathing, so I caught my breath and tried to go back to sleep. But every few minutes I would look over to see how he was doing. Of course, he was sound asleep.

At five a.m., Cal woke up, looked over at me, and said, "Good morning, Greg. How'd you sleep?" Of course, I had not slept a wink. By the time we got on the bus and to the presentation, I could hardly keep my eyes open. When Cal asked why I was so tired, I finally got enough nerve to share what happened. He laughed and said, "Oh yeah, I forgot to warn you about that when we first met." To this day, we still laugh about it.

Testifying to the United States Surgeon General was a fun experience. It also helped me realize that Utah was not the only state in trouble with youth suicides and suicides in general. I had the chance to meet remarkable people such as Colonel David Litts of the Surgeon General's staff of the Air Force.

He is one of the best and brightest suicide prevention and public policy experts I have ever had the chance to work with. He was involved in helping the Air Force achieve their success in dealing with suicide prevention. I was so impressed with him that we asked him to be our keynote at our annual suicide prevention conference, and he did a great job.

We have stayed friends through the years in our battle against suicide.

EXPERIENCING MORE CHANGE AT THE TOP

One Sunday afternoon after I had returned from the suicide prevention presentations, I received a call from my superintendent. He asked me to come down to the district office. Once again, I thought I was in trouble. When I got to the office, he was packing up stuff. I asked what he was doing, and he said, "I've been offered the position of superintendent in another school district."

I about fell out of my chair. He had just been named superintendent of the year in Utah and was a national finalist. Everyone loved working with him. I didn't think he would leave, because things had been going so well. While I talked with him, he made a comment that surprised me. He said, "It's time to move on."

He shared his appreciation and then gave me advice and wished me well. We visited for a few more minutes and then he moved on. This was my fourth superintendent. It had taken me years to convince him to allow the district to become even a little involved in suicide prevention.

Once again, we had change at the top. The assistant superintendent was appointed as the new superintendent of our school district. Before becoming the assistant superintendent, she had been an elementary principal, where my wife was her PTA president, and then a high school principal where my kids attended school. She was beloved by the teachers and was a person who got things done.

We were close as professionals and I was looking forward to working with her.

Over the last few years, I had the chance to work with her on major projects. In fact, she always invited me to learn about her position and to work together on assignments.

She was sharp and a change agent. I thought I could convince her to allow me to do more with prevention, but I was wrong. She was focused on test scores and everything we did revolved around school, district, and state testing. I enjoyed working with her, but once again, establishing mental health experts within the school system took a back seat.

She had her priorities and knew where we needed to be academically as a school district. I did all that I could to support her in her position. However, I still felt like the district needed to address the mental illness challenges we were facing in our community. When I brought up the subject with her, she agreed that it was important to be aware of, but she reminded me that "it was not our responsibility and not her priority, nor should it be mine."

So suicide prevention was moved to the bottom of my goal sheet for the year. In fairness, she was right in that I was responsible for a lot of programs and schools, and they all took time and effort to be successful. I was not angry, just stifled in wanting to do more for suicide prevention.

Handling an Unforeseen Suicide

A month later, the Provo Police Department called and asked me to come immediately to one of our middle schools. They mentioned that one of our middle school students had tried to take his life by jumping off the school's roof. I immediately drove the five minutes to the school to see fifty or so kids standing around the building.

The student had been struggling with family issues. He was a bright boy who had become lost in the shuffle of life. He had told friends to meet with him after school, right outside of the building. He said he was going to surprise them.

Unknown to everyone else, he had gotten to the roof by climbing up a drainpipe. He then ran the full length of the flat roof and jumped Superman-style onto the asphalt below, in front of the students. While he did not die, his injuries would be lifelong, and the trauma to his peers was devastating.

Because of the traumatic experience, we had to provide additional support to help the students. It was difficult for everyone involved, including the staff, who felt responsible for not preventing it. We reminded them that it was after school and no one was aware of what he had schemed.

Once again it was a deadly reminder of the things kids were struggling with in our community—stress, mental illness, bullying, and loneliness, to name a few. I was also reminded that not every suicide is preventable. However, this suicide made me even more determined to pursue suicide prevention to save as many lives as possible.

Months after the incident, I met with the student and his grandfather. The parents were devastated. Their son was still struggling despite the period of recovery. It was obvious he would need lifelong support.

While I was visiting with him, I asked why he jumped off the roof. I thought he would tell me that he wanted to die. Instead, he informed me that he thought it would be a cool way to go out in style and a way to impress his friends.

His grandfather then said, "My grandson has always been impulsive, and he drives us crazy. He cannot sit still. He was diagnosed with ADHD at a very young age." He went on to tell me that his grandson had been depressed and feeling like no one liked him and that he was a burden to the family. As he walked out the door that morning to go to school, George's last statement to his grandfather was, "I will never amount to anything anyway, so why care?" While the grandfather was worried about him, he had heard it before and thought his grandson was just having a bad day.

It was heartbreaking to see this family and this boy in so much pain.

☼ LIFESAVER ☼
IMPULSIVE BEHAVIOR, ADHD, AND SUICIDE

Impulsive behavior has several definitions, but the definition that relates most to suicide is a having a "predisposition toward rapid, unplanned reactions to internal or external stimuli without regard to the negative consequences of these reactions."[2]

In most cases, "the most likely cause of impulsive behavior is attention-deficit hyperactivity disorder, or ADHD,"[3] a disorder that makes it difficult for individuals to focus, practice self-control, or think before they act, to name a few skills ADHD affects.

Over time, I have seen more and more young people struggling with ADHD. Though the exact percentage differs depending on how ADHD is measured, the American Psychiatric Association has stated that 5 percent of children have ADHD, and that number has continued to grow.[4] Experts have shared with me that ADHD is one of the most common conditions that children struggle with.

Those with ADHD are more likely than those without ADHD to develop other mental health and behavioral issues, as well as anxiety, depression, and self-injury.[5] These are similar to the issues found in suicidal individuals.

ADHD also often increases impulsivity, which is an often-overlooked risk factor for suicide. Remember that for most people who attempt or die by suicide, they did not make the decision impulsively; however, suicidal people do lean more toward impulsivity than those who are not suicidal.[6] Just because someone is impulsive does not mean they will eventually attempt suicide. Many different factors build into losing a life to suicide; they are not spur-of-the-moment decisions or come out of the blue.

The research about suicide and ADHD or impulsivity is split. Research results suggest that there is a connection between ADHD and suicidal behavior among teenagers,[7] while other research suggests that impulsive individuals are more likely than individuals who are not impulsive to act on the feelings or thoughts of suicide.[8] Even though there is not enough evidence to build a strong association between impulsivity and suicide, it is important to be aware of the possible connections.

CALL TO ACTION

Though not all children who have ADHD attempt suicide, it is important to recognize the disorder early and get your child the help he or she needs. If you feel like your child has ADHD, have him or her evaluated by a doctor or professional therapist. If your child is diagnosed with ADHD, I encourage you to learn all that you can about impulsivity and suicide prevention.

NOTES

1. This study can be found at D. Gray, M. Moskos, and T. Keller, *Utah Youth Suicide Study New Findings* (Proceedings of the American Association of Suicidology Annual Meeting held on April 25, 2003, in Santa Fe, NM).

2. F. G. Moeller, E. S. Barratt, D. M. Dougherty, et al., "Psychiatric Aspects of Impulsivity," *American Journal of Psychiatry*, 158 (2001): 1783–93; cited at "What Is Impulsivity?" International Society for Research on Impulsivity, accessed February 26, 2018, http://www.impulsivity.org.

3. Amanda Morin, "Understanding Your Child's Trouble with Impulsivity," Understood. org, accessed February 26, 2018, https://www.understood.org/en/learning-attention -issues/child-learning-disabilities/hyperactivity-impulsivity/understanding-your-childs -trouble-with-impulsivity.

4. "Attention-Deficit/Hyperactivity Disorder (ADHD)," Centers for Disease Control and Prevention, accessed February 26, 2018, https://www.cdc.gov/ncbddd/adhd/data.html.

5. Child Mind Institute (an Understood founding partner), "Does ADHD Raise the Risk of Mental Health Issues?" Understood.org, accessed February 26, 2018, https:// www.understood.org/en/learning-attention-issues/child-learning-disabilities/add-adhd /does-adhd-raise-risk-mental-health-issues.

6. April R. Smith, Tracy K. Witte, Nadia E. Teale, Sarah L. King, Ted W. Bender, and Thomas E. Joiner, "Revisiting Impulsivity in Suicide: Implications for Civil Liability of Third Parties," *Behavioral Sciences & the Law* 26, no. 6 (2008): 779–97, as found on NCBI, accessed February 26, 2018, https://www.ncbi.nlm.nih.gov/pmc/articles /PMC2597102.

7. I. Manor, I. Gutnik, D. H. Ben-Dor, A. Apter, J. Secer, S. Tyano, A. Weizman, and G. Zalsman, "Possible Association between Attention Deficit Hyperactivity Disorder and Attempted Suicide in Adolescents—A Pilot Study," *European Psychiatry* 3 (April 2010): 146–50, as found on NCBI, accessed February 26, 2018, https://www.ncbi.nlm.nih .gov/pubmed/19699060.

8. J. J. Mann, C. Waternaux, G. L. Haas, K. M. Malone, "Toward a Clinical Model of Suicidal Behavior in Psychiatric Patients," *American Journal of Psychiatry* 156, no. 2 (1999): 181–89, as found on NCBI, accessed February 26, 2018, https://www.ncbi.nlm .nih.gov/pubmed/9989552.

CHAPTER 11

A Program to
Teach Everyone

If we were going to make a difference in the school system, we needed to begin educating and partnering with the community at large, beyond the members of the community task force and crisis team. We had started to break down the "silos," or the parts that weren't communicating or working together, within our system, so the timing was perfect. It also helped that I was on the city council and was well connected with the mayor. I had preached suicide prevention for many years, so everyone knew my passion.

The challenge once again was helping everyone to understand the importance of coming together to save lives. While folks were kind and considerate, it was difficult to convince average citizens that they could make a difference. We had to find a way to help people understand that suicide prevention meant everyone working together.

After the past suicide attempt, the community task force spent months researching suicide prevention programs from across the country. Up to this point, we had been training as best as we could based on what we were learning, but we wanted to find a program that was easy to teach and easy to understand so we could train as many people as we could as fast as we could.

We eventually found QPR, a program out of Spokane, Washington. The founder, Paul Quinnett, was a mental health administrator who had created a program that was powerful and effective, yet easy to understand. It was the CPR of mental health.

Q stands for *question*. The program teaches you how to ask questions of the person struggling. Remember, we learned that kids don't want to die; they want the pain to go away. We also learned that eight out of ten people who take their lives by suicide give a warning sign beforehand.[1] Asking the right questions is critical for those who are struggling.

P stands for *persuade*. Once you ask the tough questions about suicide, the next step is to try to persuade them to get help. We train everyone to try to convince the struggling person to talk to a professional and to offer to accompany the struggling person to wherever they decide to get help.

R stands for *refer*. If a struggling person refuses to go with me, I am going to give him or her as much information and resources as possible, including websites, mental health agencies, and crisis lines—anything that might help.

We set a goal to train one thousand Provo residents on suicide prevention using the QPR program. We set up training throughout the community. We were out evenings and Sundays, and we attended any event where we could get invited to give a presentation. The Rotary and Kiwanis clubs were always on our schedule. We also trained over seven hundred scout leaders.

The training was well received by the community. Word spread among church leaders of all faiths and among other organizations that we were willing to do suicide prevention presentations for free. As of 2017, we have trained over forty-five thousand people.

I was grateful for the support and positive feedback from many of our leaders.

As the Provo City Police Chief, I was grateful for the work that Dr. Hudnall and his team of volunteers did with the HOPE initiative with community mental health, specifically suicide prevention, intervention, and postvention. Because we all worked as a team, great things happened. Many lives were saved, and help was delivered because a community came together to help one another.

Rick Gregory
Provo City Police Chief

❍ ❍ ❍

Comment from a concerned parent:

I was at the suicide prevention training last night. Wanted to say thanks for helping me understand the warning signs and most importantly for giving me permission to ask my son if he was suicidal. I have been concerned about him for the past few days. In fact, that is why I attended the training.

After the meeting I went home and asked him about it. He started to cry and then I cried. We had a great heart-to-heart. I learned things about him that I was not even aware of. He learned that I love him unconditionally and that I am not ashamed of what he is going through. I learned that he had a plan to commit suicide the very next day. I would not have believed it if I had not heard it from him. Thank you for the work Hope4Utah [what we named our nonprofit suicide prevention organization, which is named after our task force] is doing. You are making a difference in this state. One child at a time!

❍ ❍ ❍

The experience I gained as a member of the Utah County Hope Task Force was invaluable for several reasons. First, the discussions and training gave me a very clear understanding of how to recognize and respond in a positive and correct manner to potential suicide. Second, it allowed me, through my association with the Utah National Parks Council and Boy Scouts of America, to make this training available to over eight hundred scouts and leaders. Third, it let me be much more watchful in my immediate neighborhood and family. It was not long after being trained that I had the opportunity to help prevent a serious end result. There are no words that can describe the fear of potential and the joy of prevention.

Tom Powell
Past Scout Executive
Utah National Parks Council

☻ LIFESAVER ☻
Train for Suicide Prevention

Whenever I do QPR training, I always start out by asking the audience, "How many of you are CPR certified?" Invariably, ten or fifteen people raise their hands. When I ask them why, they say because it helps saves lives.

The QPR method is also here to save lives. Though there are several different suicide prevention programs, I love QPR because it is simple, easy to understand, and easy to use. Other resources are also available.

Call to Action

Find a way in your community to become trained for suicide prevention. For QPR, use their website (qprinstitute.com) to find an instructor near you or to become certified as an individual. With the Suicide Prevention Resource Center, you can take online classes on their website (sprc.org).

There are also many other wonderful suicide prevention programs. See what your community offers and get trained. No matter what resource you use, becoming trained in suicide prevention is a valuable tool that helps save lives. The more people who are trained, the more we are all able to prevent suicide.

Note

1. K. J. Hollaway, "New Research on Epilepsy and Behavior" (New York: Nova Science), quoted on "Suicide," MHA (Mental Health America), accessed February 26, 2018, http://www.mentalhealthamerica.net/suicide#ref 2.

CHAPTER 12

Community Collaboration Makes the Difference

The more we met and trained as a community task force, the more word got out that we were involved with suicide prevention. People from all walks of life wanted to get involved in our movement. We did not recruit; we never had to, because the majority of the people on our team were professionals and connected throughout the city. They would share with a colleague or friend what they were doing, and next thing you know, I was getting a phone call.

On our community task force, we had parents who had lost a child challenge us to add support to families of suicide. One such parent was Charn. She was the wife of one of my college buddies, who was also the Utah Adjunct General. They had lost a son to suicide and were passionate about helping other families who had lost a child. These three parents who had lost children, Charn, Jackie, and David, were so dedicated. They fought hard to convince us to create a support group.

So we did. A group of eight families who had lost children developed a bookmark with their phone numbers and email addresses. They put this in a basket with other helpful information and resources. After a suicide, they would visit the home and give the basket to the family. They would then let the family know that they "understood the pain they were dealing with and that when the funeral was over and friends and family were gone, they were there to help."

They met once a month at the hospital. It was a great program, and they helped many families who had lost a family member to suicide. Having a person to talk to who understands what you are going through can be extremely helpful to the healing process.

We also were challenged to bring more awareness to the community by holding an annual "suicide walk." Two volunteers greatly helped with the first walk and with following walks: Amanda led the charge and Kari supported the effort. We brought hundreds of local folks who had lost a family member together to bring awareness to the pain and suffering—and most of all, to try to prevent it from happening again.

Appreciating Partnerships and Volunteers

Early in the process of involving the district in suicide prevention, I was getting a lot of support and attention from the state Office of Education. Anytime there was a need for help in a district, the state office would have them call me. If it happened during the day, I would take time off by using my vacation days.

At the statewide director of student services conference, they asked me to present to all the other school district directors. We were all friends, and it was comforting to share with them what we were doing. Many expressed that they could not get the support or partnership that we had. For whatever reason, the community collaboration would not work.

In fact, a director I had a good relationship with and respected shared with me afterward that he had met with his superintendent to see if their district could sponsor the same model ours had. His superintendent said, "No way are we going to waste our time with that stuff. We have more important things to focus on, like improving attendance and test scores." How disheartening!

That same year, I was at a state conference sponsored by another state agency to address drugs and alcohol. During one of the breakout sessions, we had a discussion about the role of the state agencies and the role of the school districts. It was a lively debate. Toward the end of the discussion, one of the state agency folks said, "We'll never resolve the issues we are facing in our state and communities until we all find a way to work together. The silos are killing us." He was right. It seemed like everyone from the schools and the state agencies wanted to isolate themselves and focus on their own problems in their own way instead of collaborating.

As I sat there, I thought about what he had said. Many others in the room agreed with him, and then it became almost a blame game on who was willing to partner and who wasn't. At least in Provo we had amazing community support. I just needed to figure out a way to get the district on board.

One example of someone from the community who was willing to work together for suicide prevention was Reverend Dean Jackson of the Assemblies of God. In Provo, he and his church members were some of the most willing people of anyone we worked with to volunteer and help. They not only preached serving and loving others, but they also practiced it. Time and again I would see his flock of members helping out and making a difference in the work we were doing.

I remember Reverend Jackson's help during a response to a school suicide. The community crisis team was inundated with parents wanting to know what happened with all the fire trucks and police cars out front. There were so many parents in their cars pulling into the school parking lot that it was chaos for the first responders. The poor principal was doing all she could to help even as parents were yelling at her.

I should mention that Reverend Jackson is a big guy. He is over six feet tall and fills the entire doorway. During this response, he could see what was happening and that we were losing control of the situation. He walked over to the front door of the school and filled it with his frame, stopping parents from coming in.

He helped calm the parents as they came to the door, and he let them know that the crisis team was handling the situation. He also let them know that they were blocking the entrance and the exits. He asked them to please go home, and he told them that the school would let them know if they were needed. He was awesome. I also realized the value of having the help of someone from the community. People respected him and felt comforted having a member of the community telling them that everything was under control.

Reverend Jackson's background probably helped people calm down. Before coming to Utah, he had been with the FBI in Wyoming, so he was skilled in dealing with a crisis. Beside being the pastor of his church, he was also the chaplain for the police department. He was a great asset to our community team because, when he would get a call about a suicide, he would remind dispatch to call me as well.

Responding to such calls was often difficult. Many times I would be there with the police and with the body. It was hard, but it gave us a head start to roll out the community crisis team. I know from personal experience that it also helped the family deal with the fallout after a suicide. We were experienced enough that when we showed up, we knew who to call to help volunteer to clean up and provide ongoing support for family members.

I cannot say enough about the "cleanup" crew after a suicide. It is difficult to explain the damages that are left. These volunteers showed up at all hours with their own cleaning equipment to scrub walls, clean carpets, and do their best to remove any signs of suicide.

I am proud of these "quiet heroes of the night." Members of all denominations came together to make a difference. A call would go out and dozens would show up with a mop, a bucket, and other tools. No one ever complained, and no work was ever avoided.

I remember one suicide that was especially difficult. It was midnight before these amazing people were called, and yet they all showed up. They spent over seven hours of their time and energy scrubbing, repairing a wall, and replacing carpet. Throughout the night, phone calls were made to friends who could do drywall and painting, and a call even went to a store owner, who opened his store for supplies.

No bills were left, nor money exchanged. The people who came did it out of love and support for a neighbor who lost a child. I would experience it time and again, and it always amazed me.

Comforting Others

While I was honored to be a "co-team leader" for the community crisis team, it was taking a toll on me emotionally. Words cannot express the turmoil of pain and anguish that someone experiences with the loss of a child, and I saw it again and again.

I remember meeting with one mother who had lost her only child. She was in her living room with people doing their best to comfort her. There must have been twenty adults in that room, holding her hands, whispering to her. Out of the corner of my eye I saw the husband back in the corner, just sitting in a chair, looking at the ground. Every single person in the room was sobbing except the father.

I wandered over to where he was, and as I did, he looked up at me with the most hurt and pain in his eyes that I have ever seen. I visited with him for a moment and then asked if he wanted to go outside, which he readily agreed to. We went out and sat on the steps. Nothing was said for at least five minutes. In fact, two or three people came and went during the time we sat there.

Finally, he looked over at me and asked, "Why would my son want to kill himself?"

I replied, "I don't know, except maybe he was in so much pain, he just wanted it to stop." I had found out that his girlfriend had broken up with him the night before the suicide. Maybe he was struggling with other challenges that no one was aware of.

The father then said, "Will he go to hell?"

I looked over at him and replied, "I don't think so. I think a kind Heavenly Father will look down and see that he was in so much pain and have mercy on him and on the rest of us."

He started to cry and then it turned into a sob. He looked over at me and said, "I loved that boy. I loved being with him. We went camping, hunting, and fishing together all the time. I am going to miss him. To be honest, I hurt so bad that I feel like I just want to die to be with him."

We cried together.

Recognizing the Concern with Social Media

People always wonder, "Why suicide? Why would someone take their own life?" In the many suicides I have been involved with, parents always question why their children killed themselves. In all the training I have led in schools, churches, communities, and anywhere and everywhere else you can think of, someone in the audience will almost always ask, "What do you believe is the root cause of youth suicide?"

As a first responder, I have had the chance to read many notes left by young people. In many of these notes, they will say something about not wanting the parents to blame themselves or think the suicide was their fault. The notes will then mention feeling like being a burden or not being able to deal with the pain. And in many cases, the young person mentions something about "feeling all alone" or that "no one understands what I am going through."

While suicide is complex and individualized, and we know that most people who attempt or die by suicide are struggling with a mental illness, social media is the major concern that scares me the most. I also believe social media has one of the greatest impacts on youth. I have witnessed the challenges social media and the internet can put on our young people. It does not help the loneliness nor the lack of connections.

In an article in *The Atlantic*, the author makes the point that even though we live in a time and age where communication is instant and people are always accessible, people still feel isolated. According to the article, people who spend their time on devices and social network sites find themselves lacking the skill to communicate in person. It shows how social media has taken over people's lives. It also speaks to how we can have thousands of friends but still be all alone.[1]

I saw this in the students we lost to suicide. After the suicide of a young man, I visited with the mother. She was struggling with his loss. When we visited her, she said, "I don't understand what happened to my boy. In the note that he left, he kept mentioning that he felt 'all alone.'" She then shared that he was one of the most popular kids around. He was always getting phone calls and messages on his phone and computer. By all appearances, he wasn't lonely, yet he was. It broke my heart to see his mother struggling to understand a little of what her son had been going through.

☉ LIFESAVER ☉
SOCIAL MEDIA AND
THE INTERNET

Though there is much debate as to whether social media and the internet play a role in suicide, many studies are finding that pro-suicide behavior could be linked to social media and internet use.[2] Evidence can be seen in the following ways:[3]

○ The great amount of incorrect or pro-suicide information available to anyone, anytime through the internet. This easy availability is particularly dangerous for people who are already vulnerable. They may not have ever seen the content otherwise.

○ The use of social media to cyberbully others, which has been found to increase negative feelings in those who are already suffering from mental illness or other stressors or who are already contemplating suicide.

○ The information and videos online that describe how to die by suicide, which can be viewed by anyone and may especially harm those who are already struggling.

○ The use of social media to leave suicide notes, which could negatively influence those who come across them.

○ The practice of "vamping," which is staying up all night simply to check up on friends via social media.

Think about it. Any child can use their cell phone to watch violent or pornographic movies that just a few years ago you and I would have had to use an ID to view. Young children are being exposed to more information, good and bad, at a faster rate than ever before.

So what can we do to help our children maneuver through the world of social media and the internet? Parents always ask, "Should I take away my child's phone?" I don't expect parents to take away their children's phones, unless they have abused their privileges.

However, a child does need to learn how to use social media and the internet in a positive way, and I would rather have parents instructing them than someone else. The importance is having a balance between giving your children freedom and monitoring their technology use, and a balance between using technology and being in the "real world." Finding those balances can lead to a more open relationship between you and your children.

Call to Action

Here are my suggestions for keeping your child safe while online:

○ Don't purchase a phone for your child until they are old enough to be responsible with it.
○ Put parental controls on your child's phone. Build that fence for them with controls on where they can go online. There are many apps that help you build that fence.
○ At a certain time each night, have your child turn in his or her phone to you.
○ Keep phones and technology off during dinnertime (this goes for kids and parents). That time is better spent building relationships with family members.
○ Use a tracking device on your child's phone.
○ Get help from apps, such as Bark, that alert parents if any online behavior points to suicide, cyberbullying, and other dangerous situations.

Although taking the above suggestions can help you feel better about your child's online safety, it's important to give your child some freedom and to not break his or her trust by using the suggestions to simply spy. However, if you suspect your child is having suicidal thoughts or visiting unapproved websites, intervene immediately.

Notes

1. Stephen Marche, "Is Facebook Making Us Lonely?" *The Atlantic* (May 2012), accessed March 3, 2018, https://www.theatlantic.com/magazine/archive/2012/05/is-facebook-making-us-lonely/308930.
2. David D. Luxton, Jennifer D. June, and Jonathan M. Fairall, "Social Media and Suicide: A Public Health Perspective," *American Journal of Public Health* 102, suppl. 2 (2012): S195–S200, as found at NCBI, accessed February 26, 2018, https://www.ncbi.nlm.nih.gov/pmc/articles/PMC3477910.
3. Bulleted list adapted from information from "Social Media and Suicide: A Public Health Perspective."

CHAPTER 13

Unique Obstacles in Every Suicide

When you are in a crisis, it is easy to make mistakes, and trust me, I made a lot of them. One of our worst mistakes early on occurred while helping with a suicide that happened out of our district. The school had forgotten to take the student's name off the attendance rolls. Every day for a week, the school automation system would call and inform the parents that their child was absent from school.

The father of the child called to inform me of what had happened. He told me that every night his wife would turn on the answering machine, and when she heard that message, she would run into the bedroom crying. I promised him I would get the school to fix it. It was a sad mistake on our part.

But we learned from our mistakes. From working on the community crisis team, I learned that no two suicide situations were the same. Unique obstacles always jump out at you. I would get a call from the police that there had been an attempt or a suicide and I would think that we would be able to handle it like the last one. But then something would spring up and throw us for a curve.

One of those instances occurred after a young man had taken his life on a school campus, out by the playground. By the time I got there, there were police cars and ambulances and television crews everywhere. When I walked up, everyone looked to me to handle the commotion. I started giving out orders to try to calm the situation.

We had a school to run and students to take care of, and I needed to get everyone off the campus, especially the camera crews. I did not want any student to be interviewed without a parent's permission. I also did not want to sensationalize the suicide and have it turn into a copycat.

As I gave orders and directed people off campus, everyone was supportive, except one of the camera crews. When I asked the reporter and the camera person to leave with all the rest, they snuck around and tried to get footage inside the school, where the secretaries were crying and the students were upset. The lunch lady saw them and called me for help. I was appalled. Once again, I asked them to leave the campus. They could be on the sidewalk, but not on our campus.

Unknown to me, this television crew went into a house that was being built next to the school property, right next to where the medics were responding to the youth. The crew set up their camera in the second-floor window of this house.

When someone noticed it, they asked me to try to stop it. By this time, I was tired of these idiots and responded that there was nothing I could do. They were off our campus. I couldn't believe the lengths the camera crew was going to just to get some "juicy" footage.

Thankfully, we did not have that problem with every suicide, but there were steps we took with every suicide. I would go with the school principal to the home of the victim. While we had learned that this was an important step, the new focus was based on reaching out to provide our love and support. We also let them know that the district crisis team would be at the school working with students who might be struggling.

We also let the family know that we would be holding a parent meeting that night to help other parents who may be worried about their children. Anywhere from 1 to 3 percent of youth suicides are copycats, so it's important to make sure that we do everything we can to prevent other students from taking their lives.

We always finish our visit with the family with three questions:

1. Who was with your child when he or she took his or her life? (Any individual who may have been involved could be at risk.)
2. Who are your child's best friends? (Seven out of ten young people who take their life will tell a friend, and in most cases those young people will not tell an adult. This puts the friend who was told at risk because of the guilt of knowing the friend was suicidal.)
3. When would you like to clean out your student's locker? (We let the family know they could come and clean out their child's locker at a private time.)

We would then follow up with the attendance office when we got back to the school to make sure these kids were okay. If they were not at home, we would send a community crisis team member to their house to check on them. I know it helped numerous kids who were struggling and blaming themselves. In these ways, we took postvention seriously to prevent further suicides from stemming from the original.

The school parent meeting provided the parents with the knowledge of how to help their own children and what to watch for. This helped calm the parents, which in turn helped calm the students. To every parent, we give a handout explaining what normal emotional reactions look like and what to watch for, with questions to ask according to age. We also give them a paper on behaviors young people will have after an experience with trauma.

One of the challenges we ran into was the number of parents who could not attend the parent meeting the night after the suicide because of work or other commitments. One time my phone rang off the hook with people calling for a copy of the handout. Because of this, we added everything to our website, hope4utah.com. A copy of the handouts can be found under "Ventions," which stands for prevention, intervention, and postvention.

The other important issue we addressed with our website was creating a list of every mental health agency, both public and private. Many times, people don't know where to turn in a crisis, so we wanted our website to help with that issue. We researched the information and now anyone in our county can look at the website and see the provider's information. We list names, addresses, the insurance they accept, and their specialty (cutting, depression, etc.). This has been a valuable resource for families in our community. It is a lot of work keeping it updated, but it has been worth it.

BEING PUSHED OVER THE EDGE

The suicide that was one of the most difficult and which still haunts me was that of a fourth grader in my school district. This student had been struggling with a variety of challenges. The parents and the teacher did all that they could to help.

One day in April, he came out with the rest of the kids for lunch. When the bell rang, he grabbed two jump ropes and hid behind a tree. When everyone was back in the building after lunch, he climbed up on the roof of a pavilion and waited. About ten minutes before school let out, he took his life.

When he did not return to class, the principal called me, and we spent the afternoon looking for the young man. We reached out to the police and the local bussing system so drivers could watch out for him. We had everyone looking for him.

The kindergartners, who get out of school earlier than everyone else, noticed something unusual by the tree as they walked by the pavilion. They thought it was a joke and reported it to the crossing guard, who was retired and like a grandfather to the kids. He went running to the site, and as he did he was helped by a city employee who was mowing the yard. Unfortunately, it was too late.

By the time I got to the school, the police had arrived and had taped off the area. Fire trucks, police cars, and ambulances were everywhere. The SRO informed me that because no one was around when he had died, they would have to treat the area as a crime scene. He asked that I inform the school staff and try to help keep folks away.

As he and I were talking, his mother drove up and jumped out of her van, running up to the site. As she was running up the driveway, which was a good thirty or forty yards away, the SRO told me, "I don't care what you do, Greg, but that mother cannot come over here!"

I ran to her and tried to hug her and explain what was happening. I will never forget the pain and anguish that crossed her face as she learned it was her son who took his life. Her screams still ring in my mind and have been there for many years. It took all the energy I had to hold her back.

I was finally able to get help from the school secretary, who was standing in the parking lot and who knew this mother. She helped escort her to the school to let her sit down. She helped her until the rest of her family arrived.

Our community crisis team spent the next ten hours working with staff, students, parents, and the community at large. As volunteers, the community crisis team worked together in small groups, comforting students and doing all they could to help deal with the crisis.

Around seven or eight p.m., the secretary came running to get me in the school. She was headed to her car when she saw three or four men in the schoolyard with chainsaws. They were there to cut down the tree that he had used to take his life. I went running out and, thank goodness, Dr. Tuttle, who had come with the community crisis team, came with me.

As I confronted the individuals, I asked what they were doing.

One of them replied, "We want to cut the tree down so that our children aren't reminded of the suicide every time they see that tree."

I was not sure how to respond, but I felt that despite what had happened, I could not let them cut down this beautiful tree. Dr. Tuttle came to the rescue. He informed them that the tree was not a "memorial" and that if we would leave the tree alone, most of the students would return to normalcy. They were not happy, but he used his medical and mental health expertise to calm them down and they left.

I was praying he was right.

It was after midnight when we finally slowed down.

I was so worn out emotionally and physically. At about one thirty a.m., I walked behind the school and sat down against the building's cold brick wall and broke down. I sobbed and sobbed. I was so tired and worn out. I was also admitting to myself that we had lost another child on my watch and I had failed again. I was feeling so hopeless!

After a while, I heard a noise and looked up to see the assistant superintendent, Dr. Merrill. He had come to the school to see how we were doing. He had been looking for me and was told that I was outside somewhere.

He sat down next to me and started to cry. We did not say a word to each other for nearly ten minutes. At one point, he reached over and held my hand. He and I had been administrators together for more than twenty years, so we knew each other well. He then looked at me and said, "Tell me what you need to do to prevent something like this from ever happening again. I don't care what it takes; do all that you can to prevent the next one." He also gave me permission to include the community crisis team with the school district team.

Throughout my career in academics, I have worked with seven different superintendents. All were talented and gifted in numerous areas. With each one, I had to find a way to help them understand the importance of partnering with the community in suicide prevention. Unfortunately, in almost every case, it was the loss of a student and not my proposals that helped them see the need for the district to do more.

In this case, once again it was a crisis and the loss of a child that finally got me "permission granted" to allow us to do the right thing with suicide prevention. While I wanted to yell and scream in frustration, I was grateful that we could move ahead with the partnership. The schools needed these mental health experts more than ever!

The next day, we had the community crisis team at the school working with teachers and the administration. During lunch, Dr. Tuttle asked me to walk with him out to the pavilion and the tree where the student had taken his life. As we were standing there, I noticed some kids playing soccer. One of the young men, probably the same age as Trevor, kicked his ball by the tree.

The boy ran over and grabbed his ball, then came up to us. He reached out and put his hand on the tree and asked, "Is this the tree?" Dr. Tuttle walked over to him and said, "Yes, it is." The boy looked at the tree again and then took off and went back to playing soccer.

The tree still stands. For me, it stands as a reminder to continue spreading suicide prevention so that kids can be saved instead of losing their lives to suicide. I hope it reminds other people of that too.

⊙ LIFESAVER ⊙
DOS AND DON'TS OF
REPORTING SUICIDE

As has been mentioned several times, any time a suicide or suicide attempt happened, we had to worry about copycat suicides. Why? Because coverage of a suicide can increase the risk of suicide in individuals who are already struggling,[1] depending on how it is covered, how much attention the story is given, and what is included in the coverage.

Unfortunately, young people are at risk for attempting suicide after another young person dies. Sometimes, just finding out about a suicide (the method used or the circumstances) initiates copycat behavior in a vulnerable individual, because the individual was already feeling suicidal. Suddenly, the vulnerable individual is provided with a realistic suicide method and becomes convinced that he or she can follow through with the act. Youth are especially influenced by media presentations of suicide and are more likely than any age group to die in copycat or cluster suicides (multiple suicides that occur closely together in terms of time and place).

The key word is "vulnerable"; again, talking about suicide will not plant the idea of suicide in someone's head. But it is important to be careful how we report on suicide to protect those who are already struggling and vulnerable. Covering a suicide is an opportunity to provide correct, helpful information to enable others to understand suicide and find help.

CALL TO ACTION

Whether you are a news reporter, parent, teacher, church leader, or something else, you may be faced with talking about a suicide. Learn how to best report to the group of people you are addressing. Ask your local press to follow the safe ways to report a suicide by following the guideline at suicide.org.

As you answer questions and discuss what happened, keep the following tips[2] in mind:

- **DO** give correct information without using flashy or strong words to sensationalize the suicide. **DON'T** give the story prominence, keep repeating what happened, or use flashy or alarming words.
- If using pictures in your report, **DO** use family photos or logos of suicide prevention organizations and hotlines. **DON'T** use pictures or videos of the place of the suicide, including anything graphic or people grieving.
- **DO** add warning signs, resources to use, and other helpful information in your report. **DON'T** say that the suicide came "without warning," as that is not usually the case and only stands to cause undue alarm.
- **DO** remember that suicide is a public health issue and report it as such. **DON'T** report the suicide as if it were a crime someone committed or occurred only because of a breakup or lost job.
- **DO** use quotes and statistics from experts in suicide prevention. **DON'T** include quotes from first responders on what they think happened and why it happened.
- When speaking of the person who died, **DO** use "died by suicide" or "lost to suicide." **DON'T** call the suicide a "failed attempt" or as being successful or unsuccessful.

Monitoring what is said about a suicide is an effective preventative method against copycat suicides.

Notes

1. "Recommendations for Reporting on Suicide," ReportingOnSuicide.org, accessed February 1, 2018, http://reportingonsuicide.org/recommendations/#important.
2. Compiled using information from "Recommendations for Reporting on Suicide," ReportingOnSuicide.org.

CHAPTER 14

Postvention Practices

We were now working together as a community and a school district with all hands on deck. It was refreshing to have the support. We would get the call about a suicide and Cathy would reach out to see who was available. We all had assignments. Dr. Tuttle and I were coleaders. He guided me through the process and helped me learn how to cope within a crisis.

In the meantime, we were becoming known around the state. Anytime there was a suicide and a district needed help, they would call the state Office of Education. The state office would tell them, "Call Hudnall in Provo. He will help."

And help we did. We had about forty members on our community crisis team. We had social workers, psychologists, psychiatrists, school counselors, clergy members, and law enforcement. We grew close and supported each other as a team. The strength of our team came from the members of Intermountain Healthcare and Wasatch Mental Health.

They would meet with struggling students, contact their parents, and make an appointment right then. They were talented and skilled in dealing with a crisis. I watched in awe as they helped us learn how to respond and to support those in need. It is rewarding and yet overwhelming to help someone who has lost a best friend, and in some cases, even knew about the suicide plans.

PRACTICING MORE POSTVENTION

One suicide occurred way up north in Utah, and the school did everything right to prevent it. The counselor called to get a parent to come to the school, but the child's parent was a single mother who worked on an assembly line and could not miss work.

The counselor followed proper protocol and had the girl wait in her office. It was still early in the day. After about two hours, the counselor had to go teach a class. She walked the girl down to her homeroom and privately asked the teacher to keep her eyes on her.

About twenty minutes later, the girl asked the teacher if she could go to the bathroom. Because the bathroom was across from her room, the teacher told the young lady she would wait for her outside the door. The girl went into the bathroom, took her belt off, and took her life. The suicide was devastating to the small rural community.

The community crisis team responded, and we spent a lot of time helping students, staff members, and families. It was extra difficult for the teacher, who blamed herself. But it was not her fault, and she was doing everything she could to help.

After this, Dr. Tuttle trained me to be more aware after a suicide. We knew that the risk of suicide was high after you lose someone, and even for the first responders to suicides. Some students are on the edge and something like this could set them off. It was important to identify any of the friends of the deceased and to find out if they were aware of the suicide plan. If so, they were the ones we needed to intervene with and watch out for.

One way we practiced more postvention was changing our response to memorials after a suicide. Kids wanted to do something to honor their friend. They would hang posters for everyone to sign, wear their Sunday clothes to school, and hold candlelight vigils. We had parents show up at the school wanting to plant a tree or let loose balloons in memory of the student who died by suicide.

But they did not realize that this was causing more problems with students who were struggling. One time I was at a funeral of a student who died by suicide, and I heard a student say, "Wow, if you're going to go, this is the way to do it. Look at all the attention."

We came to realize the problem with memorials, so we decided to set up a "no memorial" policy in the district. Instead of publicly honoring the person who had died by suicide, we suggested that students share their memories about their friend in writing and turn them in to the school counselors. The counselors would review them and then we would give them to the families. This way, the students could remember their friend without causing problems for struggling students.

I went to every funeral after the policy was made. It was difficult to see the pain and anguish of the students and family members. However, at almost every viewing, the parents would share the memories written by their child's school friends, and this was a powerful healing moment.

Another important postvention practice was to allow the family to retrieve any of their child's belongings from the school. Unfortunately, after one of the first suicides I had as a high school principal, I was guilty of removing belongings before the family had the chance. A later suicide showed me how important it was to give the family that chance for closure. That time, I contacted the family and invited them to collect their child's belongings after school. The custodian and I stayed late one night as the family came and cleaned out their daughter's locker. I will never forget that experience.

The student's mom, dad, siblings, and grandparents came. The mom would remove a piece of clothing from the locker and hold it close as she smelled her daughter's memory. Everyone was crying, including the custodian and me. It was a great lesson: Allow families time to grieve and honor their child.

In addition to our postvention procedures, Reverend Jackson started doing training on suicide funerals for clergy to help the families grieve and honor their lost child in an appropriate way. It was helpful to leaders who had no funeral training or experience with suicide-related funerals. He set the tone on the importance of not sensationalizing the event. He helped us gain support and respect from many church leaders of different denominations, which pulled the community together even more to work toward suicide prevention.

Seeing the Relationship between Bullying and Suicide

A few months after the suicide up north, we lost a seventh grader. He was a student who could be challenging at times; however, instead of understanding him, many of his peers bullied him and made fun of him. Even his fellow church students made fun of him. We found out later he hated going to school and to church because of the bullying.

One Saturday, he and his peers were at a church activity that involved water. After the activity, they would change back into their normal clothes. Some of the boys decided to embarrass him in front of everyone by hiding his clothes so he had nothing to change into after he was done in the water. When he came out looking for his clothes, all the boys and girls who had participated in the activity made fun of him.

Later that evening, he came home, walked into the basement, got into his father's gun closet, and took his life.

On Monday, the community crisis team was called to action. We were able to help move the school forward to a sense of "normalcy." We spent two days at the school meeting with hundreds of struggling students.

At the end of the second day, we were debriefing as a crisis team and school administration in the conference room when there was a knock at the door. The secretary stuck her head in and said that there was a young student who was struggling, and she was wondering if someone could meet with him.

Everyone, including me, was tired, but I jumped up and said I would be glad to meet with him. I walked out and saw him waiting in a chair by the secretary's counter. He was a handsome young boy who was crying. The only room available was the nurse's room, so we went in and visited.

He shared that the month before he had lost his grandfather to cancer and was still struggling from the experience. I listened and then we had a great discussion about how wonderful his grandfather was. It was a healthy visit for both of us. We talked for about ten minutes, and then he was ready to go back to class.

I was making a note as he got to the door. He opened it and then turned back to me. He asked in this wonderful young voice, "Dr. Hudnall, are you okay?" I broke down and started to cry. I was so tired. Tired of seeing the hardships our youth were going through. Tired of watching students become lost to suicide. As the tears flowed, he shut the door and walked back to where I was sitting. As I was bent over sobbing, he patted my back and said, "It'll be okay, I promise." He was an amazing young person.

That night we held a parent meeting at the school, as we usually did after a suicide, to educate the parents on how to support their grieving child and what to watch for if they are struggling emotionally. We always want to make sure we do not have any copycat suicides or a contagion.

Thank goodness Dr. Tuttle was with me on the stand. After my presentation about suicide prevention, I opened it for questions from the audience.

One rather large, angry father raised his hand and said, "I want to know what you're doing about the bullying in this school."

Word had gotten out that the young man who had died by suicide had been bullied. As I started to respond to this father's question, Dr. Tuttle reached over, put his hand on my knee, and quietly whispered, "I'll take this one."

Dr. Tuttle stood up and asked the dad in his penetrating voice, "What are you doing about it?"

The father was surprised and a little put out. He responded, "Why are you asking me? I'm just a dad."

Dr. Tuttle put on his therapy hat and asked the father, "Do you have a child that goes to this school?"

The father replied, "Yes, I do."

Then Dr. Tuttle asked the most important question that could and should have been asked all along, before this young man had been lost to suicide: "Did your son ever bully this young man?"

The mother started to cry, and the father got upset. You could see the pain in the mother and the anger in the father.

Dr. Tuttle then said in a calming voice to all the parents in the audience, "Maybe we all should stop blaming the school or one another. Maybe we should start figuring out how we as parents can stop bullying from happening again."

There was not a dry eye in the entire audience, and you could tell that everyone was soul-searching. It was by far one of the most productive parent meetings I have ever had the chance to participate in. I owe the success to Dr. Tuttle.

☯ LIFESAVER ☯
SUICIDE AND BULLYING

Bullying and suicide have a complicated relationship. Bullying is repeated, "unwanted, aggressive behavior among school aged children that involved a real or perceived power imbalance."[1] Bullying also leads to many serious and lasting problems, including suicide. Although not every student who is bullied will attempt suicide, those who are bullied are at a higher risk of suicide; however, it's important to note that bullying is not the sole cause of suicide.[2] There are usually other preexisting factors, such as a mental illness or other stressors, and bullying was the tipping point for those individuals.

Unfortunately, many students are bullied. In fact, "during the 2007–2008 school year, 32 percent of the nation's students ages 12–18 reported being bullied."[3] However, those students who were bullied were not the only ones in danger.

Bullying has a negative impact on the bullies, those being bullied, those who are both bullies and victims, and those who see the bullying happen.[4] These negative impacts include poor attendance or school performance, violence, anxiety, and depression, which is a risk factor for suicide.[5] Bullying also increases the risk of suicide, because any feelings of hopelessness or isolation felt by individuals who are already struggling with existing stressors are amplified even more.[6]

Though all children who are bullied or are bullies will not necessarily take their life by suicide, a connection exists between bullying (including cyberbullying, physical bullying, emotional bullying, and sexting) and suicide. A report by Yale University found that bully victims were two to nine times more likely to consider suicide than non-victims.[7] In addition, a survey filled out by two thousand middle school students indicated that those who had been cyberbullied were twice as likely to attempt suicide than those students who had not been cyberbullied.[8]

CALL TO ACTION

Here are steps[9] we can take to help stop bullying:

○ Have an open discussion about bullying with your child. Make sure your child feels comfortable talking about it so he or she will tell you if bullying is a problem.

○ Make sure those who are bullied understand that it is not their fault; they didn't do anything wrong.

○ In serious cases, seek professional help for the child who is being bullied, and, when necessary, involve the school and the bully's parents.

○ Get permission from your child to be included in their social media circles. This will help you watch out for cyberbullying.

○ If your child is the bully, seek help from a professional, as bullies are also at risk.

For a great school anti-bullying program, see "Rachel's Challenge" (at rachelschallenge.org). This nonprofit organization strives to replace bullying in school with kindness.

Like suicide prevention, preventing bullying takes all of us.

NOTES

1. "What Is Bullying," StopBullying.gov, accessed February 26, 2018, https://www.stopbullying.gov/what-is-bullying/index.html.

2. Ibid.

3. R. Dinkes, J. Kemp, K. Baum, and T. Snyder, "Indicators of School Crime and Safety: 2009" (NCES 2010–012/NCJ 228478), Washington, DC: National Center for Education Statistics, Institute of Education Sciences, U.S. Department of Education, and Bureau of Justice Statistics, Office of Justice Programs, U.S. Department of Justice, https://nces.ed.gov/pubs2010/2010012.pdf.

4. "Effects of Bullying," StopBullying.gov.

5. "The Relationship Between Bullying and Suicide: What We Know and What it Means for Schools," National Center for Injury Prevention and Control: Division of Violence Prevention, accessed March 1, 2018, https://www.cdc.gov/violenceprevention/pdf/bullying-suicide-translation-final-a.pdf.

6. David D. Luxton, Jennifer D. June, and Jonathan M. Fairall, "Social Media and Suicide: A Public Health Perspective," *American Journal of Public Health* 102, suppl. 2 (2012): S195–S200, as found at NCBI, accessed February 26, 2018, https://www.ncbi.nlm.nih.gov/pmc/articles/PMC3477910.

7. Y. S. Kim and B. Leventhal, "Bullying and Suicide: A Review," *International Journal of Adolescent Medicine and Health* 20, no. 2 (2008): 133–54, accessed February 26, 2018, cited at "Bullying–Suicide Link Explored in New Study by Researchers at Yale," *YaleNews*, July 16, 2008, https://news.yale.edu/2008/07/16/bullying-suicide-link-explored-new-study-researchers-yale.

8. S. Hinduja and J. W. Patchin, "Bullying, Cyberbullying, and Suicide," *Archives of Suicide Research* 14, no. 3 (2010): 206–21, cited at Luxton, et al.

9. Adapted from information found at "Bullying and Suicide," Bullying Statistics: Anti-Bullying Help, Facts, and More, accessed February 27, 2017, http://www.bullyingstatistics.org/content/bullying-and-suicide.html.

CHAPTER 15

All Hands on Deck

Through all the suicides I was dealing with, I was starting to become a mental health expert. The more suicides I responded to, the more I learned from my mental health mentors. As we traveled together, I would constantly ask questions. I worked with students who attempted suicide and with friends and family members of those who died. Everyone was willing to guide us in the direction we needed to go.

Once, I was invited down to southern Utah by a county sheriff to help after a difficult suicide, a copycat. Two students had taken their lives and another had attempted. This was not a large community. That evening we held a parent meeting. The superintendent introduced me as "one of the leading experts in school-based suicide prevention."

I kept looking around to see whom he was talking about. It was me, and I was embarrassed and appreciative at the same time. I had a lot of respect for this fellow educator. By then I had been involved with over fifteen youth suicides as a first responder. I could run a crisis team, train a community, and speak to the press about suicide prevention, intervention, and postvention. I had done over 250 presentations across the state. I was finding my niche.

COMPLETING THE
CIRCLES4HOPE MODEL

For the last few years, I had been the one person driving everything in our community for suicide prevention, intervention, and postvention. But this was to change after an experience I had with a mother in the school district. A seventh grader had shared with friends that he was depressed and had put a plan together to take his life. The school counselor intervened and contacted the parent. When the mother arrived, she was upset and embarrassed by her child's behavior.

We advised her to get help for her son immediately and gave her a list of resources. The mother told us that her child was doing it for attention. She grabbed her son and left in a hurry. That night, the young man attempted suicide and was hospitalized.

In our next community task force monthly meeting, I related the frustration of this experience. As soon as I finished sharing the story, Doran, the associate director of the local mental health agency, said, "Next time that happens, please call us and we will send over a mental health expert to do an assessment." As soon as he finished, our police chief said, "And please invite your SRO to intervene." Then the CEO of the local hospital invited us to send struggling students to the emergency room.

That moment of collaboration and ownership of "all hands on deck" began to turn the tide for us as a community. It was no longer Provo City School District or Greg asking for a favor. It was prominent folks with a lot of clout stepping into the fray. It was the most significant impact on suicide prevention and intervention for us, and it completed our Circles4Hope model that Cathy and I had developed.

The purpose of the Circles4Hope model is to provide suicide prevention, intervention, and postvention for the community, and its effectiveness depends on the involvement of community connections, mental health partnerships, and school programs.

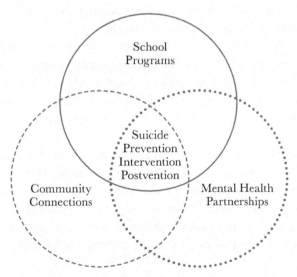

Our crisis team had started out with the community circle, because that is who we are. The players in our community circle included city leaders, religious groups, the health department, the police force, the fire station, the Boys and Girls Club, the Boy and Girl Scouts, city league coaches, and many more.

When I was on the city council, I would hear people come to meetings and blame "those folks." I would always wonder, "Who are those folks?"

Over time I realized that we are those folks! We are all part of a community. We needed every hand on deck to help us prevent suicide. If we didn't do something about suicide prevention, who would? I once heard a comment that more lives are saved from suicide by friends, coworkers, or family members than any professional. I was learning from the experts that we needed to train anyone and everyone in suicide prevention.

The second circle in our model was mental health experts, because it didn't do any good to identify someone struggling and not have a resource to send them to. In the public education arena, we played the game that we cannot refer for help. Years ago in my school district, we had a special education teacher tell a parent that her son was ADHD and needed a prescription and weekly therapy. The parent followed the teacher's instructions and then billed the school district.

Of course, we as a school district denied the charge, and the next thing I knew we were in court. We lost the case and had to not only pay for the services, but we also had to pay for attorney fees. It cost our district $70,000. Word spread and, because of that experience, schools clamped down on referring for support! For many years we were not allowed to offer any suggestions or ideas to struggling families.

To break this challenge, our model brought public and private mental health experts to the table and even offered them a chair. This allowed us the opportunity to have them meet with parents, make referrals, and provide support instead of having school do so. Many organizations wanted to be involved. I was grateful for the health department, Wasatch Mental Health, and private providers like the Family Support and Treatment Center, the Green House Center, and Aspen Counseling Services. These folks were private providers, but all committed to helping save lives.

Once, I had been invited to train a school district north of us on our community partnership model. No one could believe the success we were having with it in Provo. As I walked through the mental health partnership, the director raised his hand and said, "There is no way we would allow or encourage some sort of arrangement or partnership with some local mental health business or agency to promote to parents. It is illegal and could come back to haunt us!"

Of course, the twenty-five adults in the training all looked at me for a response! Thank goodness I had been standing by the door that looked out over the beautiful football and baseball field. I asked the district director, "You're telling me you would not or could not support a local community mental health provider or even a state agency to work with a parent for help with their child?"

He replied, "No way!"

I asked him to come over to the door where I was standing. I pointed to the thirty-seven signs on the field "promoting" every business that had paid money to support sports. I then asked him, "Aren't you doing it already?" He gasped and said, "Wow, I never thought of it that way, but, yes, you're right."

Mental health experts are a critical part of the model, and our community was lucky to have Wasatch Mental Health and Intermountain Healthcare on board as partners and players in our action plan. They were becoming our best friends.

The third circle and the one I was most comfortable with was, of course, the school system. Our kids spend 180 days a year with 990 hours of instruction time. Having a suicide prevention program at school is critical to preventing suicides. We also detail the importance of training every employee and staff member involved with the school in suicide prevention every three years to keep everyone up-to-date on information and procedure, especially when there was turnover.

Together, these three circles created a strong partnership toward a suicide prevention, intervention, and postvention approach. We named it "Ventions." We focused 80 percent on prevention, 15 percent on intervention, and 5 percent on postvention.

Along with our Circles4Hope model, we added the "critical next steps" in a community-wide effort for suicide prevention. Its three steps ensure that everyone has the same, correct information for preventing suicide.

The first step is developing a common language for suicide prevention, which ensures that all members of the community can communicate effectively as they strive to identify and assist those at risk. This common language should include the following:

- **Protective factors.** These are things that help prevent youth from attempting suicide.
- **Suicide warning signs.** These are signs and clues for identifying at-risk youth, such as increased withdrawal, change in appetite or sleep habits, talking about death, or seeking out items to use in an attempt (weapons, drugs, etc.).
- **Suicide risk factors.** These are personal life factors that may put individuals at a greater risk for harming themselves, such as a mood disorder (depression or bipolar disorder), substance use or abuse, a previous suicide attempt, or a family history of suicide.

The second step is establishing a common understanding of how to intervene with an at-risk individual, which ensures that members of the community can work in unison when connecting the individual with help. This common understanding should include the following:

○ Taking every suicidal threat seriously.
○ Speaking up if you notice any suicide warning signs.
○ Being willing to talk openly and appropriately about suicide.
○ NEVER acting shocked toward, arguing with, or lecturing an at-risk individual.
○ NEVER promising to keep suicidal thoughts or plans a secret.

The third step is maintaining a common knowledge of where to go for help, which ensures that all members of the community use their timely role in connecting at-risk individuals with prompt and appropriate care. This common knowledge should include the following:

○ Who should be contacted first when an individual is found to be at risk for suicide.
○ Who to contact in the event of a low-risk individual versus a high-risk individual.
○ What role each of the task force branches plays in connecting the individual with help, and how to access help most quickly by communicating within these partnerships.

After a suicide, many parents are shaken and scared, not knowing what to do. To address this challenge, we created a list of resources for parents in the community. As mentioned earlier, you can go to our Utah website, hope4utah.com, and click on "Mental Health Resources" in the bottom left corner. You will see that we have sixteen pages of mental health providers with their addresses, cost, insurances accepted, and what they specialize in. This has helped many families find help.

Our model was not that different from the basics of public health. The mental health experts we were working with had a good understanding of what needed to happen. We tried to find ways to connect it with everything else.

The last five years at the district office flew by. We had developed an impressive community task force that included the community, the school district, and mental health experts. We were meeting monthly to monitor and adjust as we moved forward, and we had added a family support group for those who had lost someone. It felt wonderful to have all the parts of our model working together toward suicide prevention.

⚓ LIFESAVER ⚓
MAKING A COMMUNITY IMPACT

While not every community will have every aspect of a suicide prevention organization, national and state organizations are available to help your community and to provide assistance in suicide prevention. If you want to learn more or get involved with suicide prevention in your community, I would encourage you to do online research to see what is available. Here are suggestions of resources to help you get started.

- Contact your local health and mental health agency to see what they provide or if they have any programs you can get involved with, such as outreach programs for families struggling with mental illness.
- Reach out to the American Foundation for Suicide Prevention (AFSP). They are dedicated to saving lives and bringing hope to those affected by suicide.
- Partner with the National Alliance on Mental Illness (NAMI). They provide support to families who struggle with the challenges of mental illness and are always looking for volunteers.
- Look into the Communities That Care PLUS program. They help bring communities together to determine their biggest challenges and methods for organizing solutions.
- Find other private agencies or nonprofits in your community.

CALL TO ACTION

Look up your local mental health and suicide prevention programs and get involved. It takes just one person to get the ball rolling for suicide prevention.

CHAPTER 16

Danger of Access to Lethal Means

One day, I received a call from one of our school psychologists asking if I could come over to his school to assist him in dealing with Brad, a fifth-grade student. When I got there, the psychologist shared that the teacher had read a comment a student had written in his daily journal about not wanting to live anymore. She was concerned about him and referred him to the psychologist. The psychologist was concerned because when he met with the student and did an assessment, he felt that he was struggling and dealing with serious issues.

During the assessment, the psychologist had asked him if he had thought about hurting himself. The student replied that he had. And even more scary was his response after the psychologist asked him, "If you were going to hurt yourself, how would you do it?" He replied immediately, "With my dad's gun." After receiving that information, the psychologist called his dad.

The reason he called me was that he was the son of a prominent member of our community. He wanted me to be there as backup and to deal with the father if he got angry. This was fine, because it was part of my district assignment to interact with the community, and as the superintendent liked to say, "It's Greg's job to deal with the angry parents!"

During our meeting with the student and with his father on the phone, the psychologist shared what he had learned. The father, a little embarrassed, shot back that he kept his guns in one gun safe and the ammo in the other, so it would be difficult for his young son to hurt himself.

The wise psychologist then asked the student how he would get the ammo to hurt himself. He said, "I have ammo under my mattress."

The psychologist asked the father to look under his son's mattress. The father did so and reported that he found five .22 bullets. The father asked, "Where did you get these?"

He answered, "Last time we were out target shooting, you laid the box of bullets on the table, and when you weren't looking, I grabbed a couple of extras and put them in my pocket."

The dad then reminded everyone that his son did not know the combination for the gun safe. The wise psychologist asked the student if he knew the combination to the safe, and Brad recited the numbers.

The dad was incredulous. He screamed through the phone, "How did you know the combination?"

He replied, "About two years ago when we were returning from target practice, you had me hold the guns while you opened the safe. I looked over your shoulder and remembered the combination." That experience opened my eyes to how important it is to keep guns and other lethal means away from those who are struggling. It also reminded me that even the young may struggle.

Once I was doing a training for 150 therapists, and when I finished, one of my friends who was in the audience came up to me. His name is Doug, and he told me he wanted to share an experience he had over the past few months.

He told me that he had been in a previous training of mine when I had discussed reducing access to guns when a person is in a crisis. He shared that he had a nephew who had served three terms in the military and was now home. The nephew had a difficult time transitioning to civilian life. Doug was worried about him and would stop by often to check up on him.

After my training about guns and mental health crises, he felt the importance of following up on his nephew to make sure he was okay. He stopped by his apartment to check up on him. As he was seated across from his nephew, Doug asked, "I'm worried about you and your depression. I'm wondering if you have thought about hurting yourself?" The nephew got up, walked to his closet, and pulled out his rifle.

As Doug sat there, he wondered if he should be worried. His nephew then emptied the gun of its bullets, including the one in the chamber. The nephew handed the gun to his uncle and said, "I had thought about it. Thanks for stopping by!" Doug went on to share with me that he was grateful that he had learned about the importance of reducing access to lethal means. He knew what worked, because he had seen it in action.

⊙ LIFESAVER ⊙
Reduce Access to Lethal Means

Whenever I mention that firearms are the leading suicide method in the US for adults and youth,[1] someone in the audience always wants to argue and accuse me of being anti-gun or against the NRA. The truth is, I own guns and I also own a gun safe to keep them locked up. But the truth is also that gun owners are at a higher risk of suicide than non–gun owners. It's not because they are more mentally ill or suicidal; it is because guns are a deadlier method.

The challenge is the availability of a weapon or other lethal mean when someone is suicidal. A lethal mean is how someone carries out suicide. Though these different lethal means vary in destructiveness, "reducing or restricting access to the lethal means individuals use to attempt suicide continues to be one of the most successful strategies in reducing suicide death."[2] When the availability of lethal means is scarce, people are less likely to die by suicide. The key is to reduce the suicidal person's access to the weapons or other lethal means when they are struggling.

CALL TO ACTION

If you or someone you know is struggling with suicidal thoughts, take the following steps to reduce the chance of suicide:

- Keep medicine locked away and don't store lethal medication.
- If you or your child needs medicine, use individual pill packets so only what is needed is on hand.
- Properly dispose of medicine that isn't needed anymore.
- Remove guns from the house while someone is struggling. Have a friend store them for you if necessary.
- Add extra locks to gun safes.

I have a friend whose father is a highway patrolman. She shared with me once that her father had an operation and was home recovering. At one point he became delusional. When he finally recovered and his wife expressed her concerns about his behavior, he had her lock up his guns in the trunk of his car and gave her the keys.

Reducing access to lethal means is an essential part of suicide prevention.

NOTES

1. "Suicide Statistics," American Foundation for Suicide Prevention, accessed February 6, 2018, https://afsp.org/about-suicide/suicide-statistics. (The statistics on this webpage were based off the "Data & Statistics Fatal Injury Report for 2016" by the Centers for Disease Control and Prevention.)
2. "Reducing Access to Lethal Means," Suicide Awareness Voices of Education (SAVE), accessed February 1, 2018, https://save.org/about-suicide/preventing-suicide/reducing-access-to-means. [Reprinted with permission from Suicide Awareness Voices of Education (SAVE).]

PART 4

The Hope Squad: Suicide Is Not an Option

CHAPTER 17

Peers Helping Peers

As expected, the loss of the fourth grader shook up the public and the district. In our next school board meeting, the board members grilled the superintendent about the loss of the fourth grader and what was being done to prevent it from happening again. One of the board members, a professor at Brigham Young University, said, "I hope this will challenge us to do more to figure out how we can help these youths who are struggling."

The superintendent replied, "It does challenge us, and I'm authorizing Dr. Hudnall to work with the district and the community to put something together and report back to the board."

There it was. We finally had permission and approval to move suicide prevention to a priority and work as a school district to put a plan together. I immediately pulled all the social workers, psychologists, and school counselors together to start figuring it out. We started meeting every month. Our first assignment was to research every suicide prevention program for schools to see what we could do to help the struggling youth.

The experience with the ninth grader who had given his watch away to a friend, saying that his family would be better off without him, reminded us that we were missing a critical piece in suicide prevention in schools. We knew we had to do something. There were other examples of times when a student had confided in a peer but an adult had not been involved.

A principal once shared that he had been at the hospital after a student had attempted suicide. Some of the student's friends were also there, and he recognized one who was having a difficult time. When he asked the young man how he was doing, the student replied, "He told me he was going to do it and I did nothing to stop him." When the principal asked why, the young man replied, "Because I thought it was my job to protect him from adults. Isn't that what we're supposed to do?"

Another example comes from a time the Provo mayor invited the community task force to do a "Town Hall" meeting on suicide. The mayor was concerned with all the youth taking their lives and asked if we could do more to help educate the community on preventing suicides. We had a good turnout. Folks were scared and wanted to know what to do. At the end of the training, I opened it up to questions from the audience.

A young lady raised her hand and asked, "My best friend told me she was going to kill herself last night. What should I do?" Here it was again, a young person trying to know what to do to protect a friend from taking her life. I told her that it was probably best to get her to an adult they trusted.

The young lady then said, "But she'll get mad at me, and I don't think I can do that."

I was frustrated because I was hearing and seeing this more and more. I replied, "Would you rather have a friend who is alive and mad at you or a friend who may hurt herself and even possibly take her life?"

The young lady teared up and said, "I don't know what to do."

These experiences with young people taking their lives after sharing with a friend that they were struggling motivated us to do more with peer-to-peer intervention and inspired us to find ways to help educate young people so they'd be able to help their peers. We met with the parents of the ninth grader who had taken his life. They were supportive about us as a school district taking on the challenge of youth suicide and finding a way to help peers become involved.

In fact, we used their daughter to help us promote the idea of peers helping peers. She was then a student at Provo High and wanted to become more involved in sharing her brother's story. She was not afraid to share that he had told friends he was struggling and not one friend had told an adult.

The more we investigated, the more we learned that most young people who died by suicide gave a warning sign or told a friend, but 75 percent of the time, the friend didn't tell an adult.[1]

As we searched for a school suicide prevention program, we came across research stating that students were more likely to turn to a friend than to an adult if they were suicidal, because they felt safer talking to a peer. For this reason, the research suggested that suicide prevention could be done by training students so they could better help their friends and peers who came to them when thinking about suicide.[2]

That was it, the missing piece! We had enough evidence, both researched and from real-life experiences, that we needed to somehow train the peers that struggling students were turning to and have those peers become a step in suicide prevention.

SEARCHING FOR A SUICIDE PREVENTION PROGRAM

Once we knew what was missing, we needed to come up with a plan. At our monthly meetings, the school district counselors, psychologists, social workers, and I came together to discuss suicide and research every program across the world to find a suicide prevention program that involved peers. While we liked certain parts of most programs, the entire team still felt that some things were missing.

For example, most programs had great starts, fun ideas, and excellent ways to bring the school together for activities that promoted suicide prevention. But none were comprehensive enough or focused on building suicide prevention, intervention, and postvention month to month or year to year in a way that guided and assisted the instructor and excited the kids. What they did was excellent—it just wasn't enough. We wanted something that would build on each lesson and that also repeated itself. We also wanted it for elementary, middle, and high school.

Many administrators and school leaders thought we were crazy for wanting help for all of our schools, including the elementary program. We heard time and again that those kids were too young and would not understand, let alone comprehend, what they were learning. However, we had had several suicide experiences with elementary students, and we knew we needed to add an elementary piece. Talking about suicide prevention for an elementary school can be scary for adults. We knew we had our work cut out for us.

Over the next year, we continued meeting to review programs, discuss ideas, and try to figure out what the next step was. We looked at everything, but we could not find a stand-alone, school-based, peer-to-peer program developed by educators. This concerned us because people outside of the school system do not understand the challenges within a school system, from class schedules to staff assignments to budget restraints. Over the years, I had heard my fellow administrators repeatedly say, "Mental health people just don't get it when they try to work with us in schools. They don't understand our culture."

However, we felt we needed both the educator and the mental health expert to bring suicide prevention together in a school: the educator because they understand the system and the culture, and the mental health expert to be sure we were teaching the right concepts about how to recognize a peer who is struggling and know what to do about it.

During our search, we occasionally came across a program that seemed like a good fit but ended up not working out. It was frustrating to find a program we liked but then discover that it didn't have all the pieces we wanted.

I saw this as a principal. My department heads would go to a conference and come back and share a memorable experience they had while listening to a speaker. They fell in love with the speaker's message and felt that we had to implement the program. They bought the speaker's book and would request to purchase the program.

To be supportive, I would pay for the program. A few months later, I would follow up and ask how it was going. Invariably, they would share their frustrations that the program did not have enough material after a one-time shot or a few months.

DECIDING TO BUILD
OUR OWN PROGRAM

Our team of counselors, psychologists, and social workers fell back on the idea of "peer to peer." Instead of focusing on leadership and role models, we needed the focus to be more on suicide prevention. We wanted a curriculum that would train the students to recognize warning signs, learn how to intervene when a peer is struggling, and, most important, show when to go to an adult.

Somehow, we needed to find a way to help these young people help their friends. Unfortunately, many peers think the best thing to do is to hide the fact that their friend is struggling. This would be our biggest challenge. How do we break that wall of silence? The more we discussed it, the more we knew that we had to do something.

I assigned the team of school district experts to spend the summer reviewing everything that was out there for schools in suicide prevention. There had to be a program that addressed our concerns. But as each month rolled by, I was finding that we had a set of criteria to meet and that although most programs touched on them, they did not address them.

Our criteria included the following:

1. Partnership with the local mental health agency
2. Peers must be nominated by peers
3. Meet weekly/monthly to train students
4. Must fit into the school schedule/system
5. Parent approval and support
6. Curriculum should build year to year
7. Programs for elementary through high school

It was seeming less likely that we would find a complete program that met our criteria and that we could implement in our own district. Finally, we decided to build our own program. While it was scary, we felt we needed something different than what was out there, but we still wanted the youth to have suicide prevention training and support. Building our own program would help us have all the pieces we wanted, but it was easier said than done.

It was 2003, and we wanted to develop curriculum for elementary, middle, and high school. It would take us ten years to finish the product.

We wanted to build the curriculum around the concept of a club or after-school program. It needed to be flexible and able to work within a school system. It needed to be easy to understand and even easier to teach. It had to focus on teaching peers how to assist peers.

We also wanted to make sure the curriculum was a continuation for the students. Our goal was fourth through twelfth grades. It was a struggle because many folks, including teachers and administrators, did not want us even mentioning the word *suicide* in the elementary grades. However, we had to remind everyone that we had lost a fourth grader to suicide.

Trying a Peer-to-Peer Program

During the time that we were looking for suicide prevention programs, we continued to be motivated by stories of struggling students.

Time and again, we heard and saw a struggling student turn to a friend or peer instead of an adult. In general, youth, especially teenagers, feel more comfortable talking about real issues with their friends.

This knowledge is one reason we decided to try peer-to-peer suicide prevention. If the kids weren't turning to adults, whom we were training in the community through our task force, then we needed to train whomever the kids were turning to.

Along with this, peers were often the first to know about stressors in each other's lives because of all the time they spend together in and out of school. They would know who broke up with whom, who was fighting with parents, who was worried about school or extracurricular activity performance, and other stressors that youth commonly feel.

It was our hope that a peer-to-peer suicide prevention program would give students a safe place to talk about their stressors and wouldn't turn to hurting themselves.

⊙ LIFESAVER ⊙
Youth Stressors and
Academic Performance Anxiety

A stressor is defined as a change of any kind that leads to someone making an adjustment in their life.[3] These changes come in many different shapes and forms for youth, including grief, family conflict or history of illness (both physical and mental), social situations, substance abuse, and violence.[4]

These stressors have the potential to push a young person who is already struggling over the edge. In fact, Dr. Jack Klott, a former therapist who spent thirty years working with depressed and suicidal clients, wrote that suicide rarely occurs outside of the context of medical mental disorders and significant social stressors.[5] Major stressors include perceived problems such as a romantic breakup, a disciplinary action, or a fear of being in trouble.

Because suicide is "multi-faceted" and very individualized, which makes it all the more challenging to prevent, it is important for everyone in that individual's life to recognize the signs that he or she may be struggling and to be aware when a major social stressor affects him or her. It may be something that seems minor to you, but it could affect them differently.

An obvious stressor in the lives of students is school. For example, one day I was contacted by a parent to see if I could come to the emergency room as soon as possible. Her son had attempted suicide and was not doing well. When I got there, I saw he was covered in blood. The parents begged for help; they did not know what to do. As I was visiting with the parents, one of our community crisis team members walked by. He happened to be a social worker for the emergency room.

I stepped aside to visit with him to find out more about this young man. The social worker gave me advice and assured me he would help the parents. He said the student would not open up in front of his parents. He also said that he had tried to kill himself with his father's gun, which was upsetting to the mother and frustrating to the dad.

I asked to meet with their son alone to see if I could gather additional insight as to what was going on. When I met with him, I could tell he had been struggling. When I asked him what was going on, he replied, "I was in so much emotional pain that I could not bear it any longer."

I asked, "What was causing the unbearable pain?"

He replied, "I had just received my report card and I had my first A- I have ever had! I feel like such a failure."

We visited for a while and then I turned the matter over to the emergency room social worker. I remember driving home thinking about this amazing young man who felt like he was a failure because of an A- grade. This was clearly a major stressor in his life that, when combined with other underlying issues, had led him to take drastic action.

Of course, not all children who receive an A- will attempt suicide. However, academic performance anxiety is one of the biggest challenges facing schools today.[6] Where does this anxiety come from? Sometimes it can come from parents. In his book *Suicide & Psychological Pain: Prevention That Works*,

Dr. Klott said that "young people who believe that affirmation and love are won and earned are the most vulnerable [to academic performance anxiety]."[7]

The child who wins your love or positive statement of achievement by earning an A grade or for being a star on the basketball team is the most vulnerable for suicide ideations, attempts, or completions in a high school setting. Life can be difficult when young people feel or believe that the only way to earn love and support is through being the best at things.

CALL TO ACTION

Though some stress is good and necessary, it's important for parents to be aware if their children are sinking in it. If you notice that your child is more stressed than usual or that stress is affecting your child emotionally, mentally, or physically, try the following suggestions[8] to help your child manage stress:

○ Encourage your child to tell you about his or her stress and listen to what is said.

○ Make sure your child understands that no matter what he or she does, you will never withdraw your love. Say, "I love you," and other words of affirmation often to your child.

○ Model positive stress management, such as taking a break from something stressful, breathing deep for relaxation, exercising regularly, and eating well, and encourage your child to do so as well.

○ Invite your child to practice stressful situations together, so he or she will feel less stressed by knowing what to expect.

Teach your child to talk positively and how he or she can feel good about doing something even if it isn't what they think is "perfect."

NOTES

1. World Health Organization, "Preventing Suicide: A Resource for Counsellors," Geneva, 2006, 17, http://apps.who.int/iris/bitstream/10665/43487/1/9241594314_eng.pdf.
2. Ibid.
3. "Teen Stressors," Cincinnati Children's, accessed February 27, 2018, https://www.cincinnatichildrens.org/service/s/surviving-teens/stressors.
4. Ibid.
5. Jack Klott, "Suicide & Psychological Pain: Prevention That Works" (Eau Claire: PESI Publishing & Media, 2012), 34.
6. Ibid., 20–21.
7. Ibid.
8. Adapted from information found at American Academy of Child & Adolescent Psychiatry, "Facts for Families," no. 66 (May 2005), updated February 2013, accessed March 5, 2018, https://www.aacap.org/aacap/Families_and_Youth/Facts_for_Families /Facts_for_Families_Pages/Helping_Teenagers_With_Stress_66.aspx.

CHAPTER 18

The Successful Implementation of the Hope Squad

After years of researching and reviewing, we had decided to start our own program. During the 2003–2004 school year, we started by focusing on Timpview High School. It was a school of twenty-one hundred students from ninth grade to twelfth grade. It was also a school that had way too many threats, attempts, and, unfortunately, suicides. It was a school where many young people felt the pressures of school and life. It was also a school that had amazing staff, caring students, and supportive parents.

The staff included Monte, the lead counselor and one of the most caring individuals I have ever met. Wendi was the school social worker, and she knew her stuff. Together they made the perfect pair to help us figure out how to help the school. We decided if we could be successful at Timpview, we could be successful anywhere.

Dr. Bayless was the principal, and he and his assistant, Brad Monks, were amazing leaders. You could tell they were tired of the suicides as much as we were. So Monte and Wendi went to every English class and asked every student, "If you were struggling and needed someone to talk to, who would you talk to? List the names of three peers you would feel comfortable talking with." Forty student names rose to the top.

The kids nominated by their peers were remarkable youth. These were the kids that friends would go to when they needed someone to talk with. Those nominated students started gathering once a month. At the meetings, they were taught how to recognize warning signs, how to listen and engage with peers who were struggling, and, most important, when to go to an adult!

The kids came up with the name "Hope Squad," the "Hope" standing for Hold On, Persuade, and Empower. Our community task force was the Utah

County Hope Task Force, so the name was perfect. They were a group of kids nominated by their peers to help their peers.

The key to the program was the nominations of the peers to the Hope Squad and the monthly training. The program at Timpview was so successful that we put Hope Squads into every school in the district: thirteen elementary schools, three middle schools, and three high schools. During training, we focused on mental wellness, resiliency, and acts of kindness (anti-bullying). I was amazed at the number of young people who were struggling. After the loss of the fourth grader on campus, we had made our commitment to do all that we could within our schools to help children feel safe and to know that there were peers to help.

With the Hope Squads in place in the schools, we started on a journey that no one would have believed was possible.

SEEING IMMEDIATE SUCCESS

The year 2004, the first year with the Hope Squads in our schools, was the first year in three years that we went without a single youth suicide in our district. While it was a small miracle, we were grateful for a respite. At the end of the school year, we held our breath and gave thanks for the many people who helped and for the lives that were saved. We were especially grateful for the Hope Squad kids; they were making all the difference. They were excited about being nominated by their peers and were working hard to help them.

We found out that the key ingredients to a successful Hope Squad include the following:

1. An advisor (assigned by the administration) who loves kids and is passionate about suicide prevention
2. A supportive principal and staff
3. Committed Hope Squad students
4. Encouraging and watchful parents
5. A community partnership with mental health agencies
6. Ongoing review and improvement according to data collection

The model was created by educators and reviewed and enhanced by mental health experts. Hope Squad students meet as either a club, class, or after-school program. We developed it for elementary through high schools. Our goal was to create a continual curriculum that students could learn each month.

The first-year curriculum included the following:

1. Having hope (understanding that Hope Squad members work with the local mental health agencies)
2. Understanding and identifying warning signs and risk factors

3. Learning how to talk to a struggling friend
4. Learning boundaries
5. Self-care
6. Helping peers who get bullied
7. Hope Week (a week designated by the school in which Hope Squad members hold activities and games during lunch hour to promote mental health awareness)

Because the community crisis team had spent the previous five years developing community partners, the Hope Squad was a natural fit for us. We had the support of law enforcement, mental health experts, and hospital folks. We had just needed a better way to identify those most at risk.

And identify we did.

It was amazing how much better we could identify those at risk with the help of their peers. Being on the Hope Squad is about caring, showing kindness, listening, empowering, and having the courage to talk to a peer. It's about being there to help a friend who is struggling and needing someone to understand what he or she is struggling with. It involves understanding the importance of when to go to an adult.

I wish every reader of this book had the chance to meet with a Hope Squad program. You would see amazing young people who feel empowered to not only help others but feel that they are making a difference with their lives. Two Timpview Hope Squad members shared with me that while they belonged to three or four clubs, they kept coming back to the Hope Squad because they felt that they were making a difference.

Hope Squad members get excited talking about what they do. While they are trained not to be counselors or therapists, they are good listeners and caring people.

One of the important pieces of the Hope Squad was working on reducing and eventually removing the stigma associated with mental illness—helping young people to understand that they are not alone in their struggles and that it is okay to get help from an adult.

Another important piece was that of creating connectedness. Too many of our youth are feeling alone, being bullied, or dealing with anxiety and other issues. We saw firsthand what a group of talented youth who are trained in how to reach out and help can do.

A wise mental health expert once said to me, "You can have a hundred kids that are struggling with depression and even suicide ideation. The amazing thing is that just having a friend, someone that reaches out to them, showing that they care and are truly compassionate, could help ninety-seven of them. The remaining three will need to be seen by a professional. But what it does show is the power of caring and connectedness." This certainly stood true with the Hope Squad kids.

The Hope Squads seek to reduce self-destructive behavior and youth suicide by training, building, and creating change in schools and communities. The members are trained to recognize suicide warning signs and act upon those warning signs to break the code of silence. The Hope Squad members build positive relationships among peers and faculty to facilitate acceptance for students seeking help.

Finally, Hope Squad members work to change the school culture by reducing stigmas about suicide and mental health. It takes two to three years to change the school culture.

What we found with the Hope Squad kids is that many of these young people were already being approached by their peers who were struggling with depression and suicidal thoughts. In the past, those kids did not know what to do to help a friend in crisis. So they listened, tried to do all they could to protect them from hurting themselves, and at times even hid the information from adults.

But with some training, they had the suicide prevention tools they needed to truly help their peers. By training the Hope Squad students, we could create a team of skilled young people who could in turn help friends who are struggling. The Hope Squad students are trained to be the eyes and ears of the school as friends who know how to help those who are struggling.

It was amazing to see the number of kids who were hurting. While only the serious referrals would be counted in our data, I was impressed with the number of peers these Hope Squad kids were helping. They were willing to reach out to anyone and everyone who was struggling. Sometimes, all a struggling student needs is to have someone notice them and reach out.

The Hope Squad kids are trained to report every concern. One school counselor / Hope Squad advisor told me that she had an eighth-grade Hope Squad student tell her that she saw a fellow student writing a very negative comment on her notebook, but she wasn't sure it was anything to worry about. The advisor brought the fellow student in and was surprised that the student had actually been thinking about hurting herself. The advisor told me that she was impressed that this Hope Squad member had taken the initiative to follow up with her concerns.

Another advisor shared that her Hope Squad had rallied around a fellow student who was being bullied on the playground at her elementary school. The advisor was impressed with how they reached out to the bully victim.

We even had an advisor share that her Hope Squad member had reported a concern about a fellow student's comment in the locker room. The advisor followed up on it with the school resource officer. The officer met with the student and found out the student had access to his father's gun. While no threat had been made, it was important enough for everyone to get involved.

The goodness continues with these young people. One young man shared that he decided that every day at lunch he would sit by a new person who was eating alone. It became his goal in life to not only meet new kids but to also be a genuine friend to others. One school set a procedure so that at the beginning of the school year, every new kid who registered for school after September was shown their class schedule by a Hope Squad member.

Even with all the success this first year with Hope Squads showed, the "naysayers" were alive and well even in the schools. I had administrators and teachers contacting me to say that we should not have programs in our school that "talk about suicide," because they believed it would increase the risk for more suicides.

Even a few of the prominent leaders, including faith-based leaders, came to my office and demanded that we stop the program immediately. If it weren't for Wasatch Mental Health and Intermountain Healthcare, we would have been in trouble. Our mental health leaders in our community took a stand on our behalf. It helped that they were part of our community crisis team and had seen all the work we had been doing to get to this point. One such supporter was Mark Payne, the superintendent of the state hospital. He was a voice of reason to many in the community who had shared concerns. He was an expert in the mental health field and was not afraid to let folks know that we were doing the right thing by involving peers.

One day, the superintendent shared concerns from the elementary folks about our Hope Squads. He informed me that some principals were concerned that we were talking about it at that age. I sat for a moment and thought about what I could say, and then I gently reminded him of our "night from hell," when the fourth grader had taken his life. He closed his eyes and leaned back in his chair.

I thought he was upset for reminding him of that terrible event. When he looked at me again, he had tears in his eyes as he said, "You do this, Greg, and if any of our administrators get in the way, please let me know and I will take care of it. I never ever want to lose another young person like that again."

No matter what people thought or what concerns they held, our first year was a success because not one student had lost his or her life. I knew we had something special because of all the calls I was getting from our community partners.

One call I received was from a doctor at the Utah Valley emergency room. His name was Dr. Keith Hooker, and he contacted me to find out about this "Hope Squad thing" that a parent had talked about to him. When I shared what it was, he said, "Good work, Greg. Please tell your task force thanks. It's about time someone came up with a great idea to help kids in this community." That comment was incredibly rewarding.

TRYING TO HELP THE LGBTQ STUDENTS

In the meantime, a group of students at Provo High School decided they wanted to bring in a Gay–Straight Alliance club. The GSA is a national organization that works with students to develop a student-run club whose goal is to provide a safe place for students to meet and support each other and to work to end homophobia and transphobia at the school and in the community.

Unfortunately, this decision resulted in a few ugly months with the school board and community church leaders. Even the students were treating each other poorly. At one school board meeting, we had two hundred people show up to argue, attack, and threaten everyone who was for the club, and they were unwilling to listen to those who were in favor of it.

Regardless of beliefs, kids need to know that they can be safe in school. I firmly believe that every child needs to be able to attend school in a safe, non-threatening environment regardless of race, religion, beliefs, or sexual identity. We may not agree with someone's beliefs, but we should always treat them with respect and dignity.

Unfortunately, one of the suicide attempts that we had the first year of Hope Squads was a young lady who wanted to be part of the Gay–Straight Alliance club at Provo High School. I was saddened when I heard she had attempted to take her life by suicide. She had been bullied over and over at school, and she finally could not take it anymore.

Even my son, who was a Provo High student at the time, came home one day and informed his mother and I that he was sickened to see how the GSA kids were being treated by their peers.

Finally, the GSA club was approved by our school board for Provo High School. Our superintendent was the one who helped everyone understand the need to calm down and try to reason with each other. Unfortunately, the damage was done, and too many kids suffered by being bullied by their peers for wanting to join the club.

⊙ LIFESAVER ⊙
SUICIDE RISK OF
LGBTQ STUDENTS

Bullying, rejection, and violence are some of the challenges that LGBTQ students face. Unfortunately, those challenges often lead to suicide. In fact, students who identify as LGBTQ are about three times more likely to attempt suicide than those who identify as heterosexual.[1]

One reason LGBTQ students have more suicide attempts could be that they tend to have more risk factors for suicide in general as well as risk factors that are more severe. These include family rejection, previous attempts, verbal and physical abuse, and existing substance abuse or mental illness. Even though LGBTQ students generally have more risk factors, it is important to remember that simply being LGBTQ is not itself a risk factor. Rather, those students experience more stressors that come with being a minority, stressors that contribute to the risk factors as well as suicidal behavior.[2]

CALL TO ACTION

Take time to become aware of the challenges facing LGBTQ youth, especially those that could prompt suicidal behavior. Some helpful sources include the American Association of Suicidology (see footnote 2) and the Centers for Disease Control and Prevention.[3]

Review resources such as the Trevor Project (thetrevorproject.org/education) to learn more about how you can help LGBTQ students. If your child is LGBTQ, be supportive and accepting of him or her. If your student attends school with students who are LGBTQ, be supportive and accepting of those students, and encourage your child to do likewise.

NOTES

1. "Preventing Suicide: Facts About Suicide," The Trevor Project, accessed March 7, 2018, https://www.thetrevorproject.org/resources/preventing-suicide/facts-about-suicide/#sm.0000y3atbabxjeq9xz51gpkzy9ymg.
2. American Association of Suicidology, "Suicidal Behavior Among Lesbian, Gay, Bisexual, and Transgender Youth Fact Sheet," 2, http://www.suicidology.org/Portals/14/docs/Resources/LGBT%20Resources/SuicidalBehaviorAmongLGBTYouthFacts.pdf.
3. Visit https://www.cdc.gov/healthyyouth/protective/pdf/parents_influence_lgb.pdf for more information.

CHAPTER 19

Positive Responses
and Results

At the end of year one, we were amazed what a difference Hope Squads had made in suicide prevention. We had done the impossible with the help of Hope Squad students, dedicated advisors, supportive parents, and, in most cases, helpful administrators.

We asked every school counselor to keep track of the students who were referred for help by Hope Squad members and anyone else who had either attempted or threatened. At the end of the year, we had fifty-six attempts. We also had hospitalized eight students who were planning to take their lives.

The community partnership was working! We would not have had the ability to get these kids hospitalized without everyone's help and support. It was year one with the Circles4Hope model and the Hope Squads working together.

As we continued to improve our program, ongoing concerns and questions rose to the top. The biggest elephant in the room was that of liability. Could a school be sued for having a Hope Squad? Could a student on the Hope Squad be sued? Our district staff was concerned about liability, and it came to my attention that I needed to address it.

It is unfortunate that our country has become so litigious. I saw it and experienced it as a principal and at the district level. We even had to take away programs and stop services because we were afraid of being sued. One of my superintendents once said to me, "Your job is to never, ever let something end up in court."

I realized the fear associated with liability. I get it. But I also knew that sometimes we need to have the courage to take that risk. I saw way too many kids dying, and I knew we needed something different than what we had.

That "something different" was having kids talk to kids, but, unfortunately, that comes with liability. Many schools were hesitant to include Hope Squads for that reason. Being a change agent and not willing to give up, I reached out to Utah State Attorney General Mark Shurtleff, and he invited me to his office in Salt Lake City.

When we first met, I was impressed with how kind and caring and interested he was. He told me that he had a daughter who struggled with depression, and he said that he wanted to help. When I described our model, he loved it.

When I shared the concerns about liability, he smiled and said, "I've never known of a school district or school employee or even a volunteer who has ever been sued for trying to help someone. But I know of at least three school districts right now who are being sued for doing nothing. I would err on the side of kids helping kids." He suggested that we add a parent permission form that explained the program and allowed the parents to make the decision about allowing their child to be on the Hope Squad.

At a subsequent meeting, he remarked that he wished his daughter's school had a Hope Squad. He went on to say that we needed more ways to help one another and more ways to educate and help parents. He said, "I'm a pretty bright guy, and these things like mental illness can be scary and overwhelming at times."

He would get more involved in suicide prevention and even spoke once at our annual suicide prevention conference. I admired his courage to speak about his daughter and the challenges they faced as a family. Everywhere we ran into each other, he would ask about the program, ask what he could do to help, and encourage me to continue the fight.

HEARING STORIES OF SUCCESS

Year two was more of the same. A student was struggling, a peer was listening, and help was being provided. Parents were contacted and given a referral to our local mental health agency.

Once a student was identified as a "High Risk" (meaning the student threatened to harm himself or herself), our school resource officer would intervene and pink slip them into custody. In the state of Utah, a police officer can take youth into custody if they are a harm to themselves or to someone else. There is an official name for this law in the books, but we have always referred to it as "the pink slip" because the form is pink.

Though we did not lose any students to suicide the second year, it was a tough year because we had over seventy attempts and another seven hospitalized. One night, I received a call about a young man who had tried to take his life. The referral was made by a friend, but it was too late. The young man had attempted and was hospitalized. Thank goodness he lived.

We also learned once again that these young people do not want to die; they want the pain to go away. You could see this by the many ways they attempted. They would take pills and then call someone. They would have a gun and then shoot themselves in the foot. They were in pain, but they did not want to die; they were crying out for help!

At the end of year two, I received the following email from a high school counselor who had received it from a student's parent. The counselor shared that she had received a referral from one of the Hope Squad members, which resulted in the email.

Dear Counselor,

I want to thank you again so very, very much for calling me today. I had a complete breakdown after we got off the phone, but then I cleared my head and life moved on. I had to do my best to not smother [my student] with hugs and kisses when he came home from school! I was helping him clean his room after school and thankfully the conversation just flowed.

Without prompt, he told me about his conversation with you today. I guess the whole situation stems from some girl vs. best friend emotion he struggled with last year. We were very aware of that situation and were happy to see him work out those feelings. I didn't realize how much that struggle affected him, though. I guess he told [a Hope Squad member] about it and [the Hope Squad member] told you. My son told me how good it felt to talk to you. He said it felt good to talk to an adult about it.

Your Hope Squad is awesome. I'm so thankful that [the Hope Squad member] takes his job seriously and that there is protocol at the high school concerning the Hope Squad. I'm so happy that there are so many great people at your school. Thank you for being proactive and for helping parents protect and encourage their kids. I feel like this was a good wake-up call for my husband and me . . . to pay a little closer attention and to never take our kids' happiness for granted.

Clearly from the amount of times I've said "thankful" in this email, I am feeling overwhelmingly thankful! Thank you so much for caring about my child and for having such a wonderful program at your school.

I wish I could share the hundreds of emails and phone calls we started to get in response to implementing the Hope Squad. From the amount of positive feedback and from the results we were seeing, I knew the Hope Squad kids were truly making a difference.

CONTINUING TO HELP STATEWIDE CRISES

During this time, we continued to get calls from around the state for help in suicide prevention and training. Youth suicides were not just happening in

Provo. When someone called, we rallied the crisis team and responded imme-diately. It was all volunteer work where we covered our own travel costs, food, and, at times, hotels. Even though I used up a lot of my family vacation time and other resources, my wife and children were supportive.

One crisis I helped with happened the day before my anniversary. I received a call from a high school principal in Moab, in southern Utah. He had just lost a student and he asked if I could help. I was torn because of the family event, but I knew I needed to help. I asked my seventy-five-year-old father to accompany me.

We jumped in my car and took off for Moab. It was a four-hour drive, and along the way we got stuck in spring construction on the highway close to Green River. As we were locked in traffic in a single lane, waiting to even move, my mobile phone went off. When I answered it, the Moab principal's voice on the other end was distraught as he said, "We just heard of another suicide attempt. Could you please get here!"

I hung up and leaned over to my father and said, "Hold on, Dad." I swerved out of the lane we were in and, avoiding cones and barrels, drove on the con-struction side of the highway. Of course, everyone was yelling and screaming at me, and my poor father was hanging on for dear life and could not believe his son would do such a crazy thing. To be honest, it was a little fun.

We passed twenty or so cars and made it back in the single lane just as the construction crew's guide car was coming the other way with his emergency lights on. He was not happy, either. We sped away, and I knew I was driving too fast, but I was thinking of that poor school in crisis. As we climbed a hill, we passed a state trooper coming the other way, and I am sure the trooper was called because of my driving.

As he went by, I looked in my mirror and saw him turn around and turn on his lights. I knew I was caught, so I pulled over and said, "Dad, don't say anything. Let's just get the ticket and get out of here." I didn't want to waste time explaining the situation to the state trooper; I just wanted to get my ticket and be back on the road.

He replied, "Son, just explain to him why you were driving so crazy and maybe he'll let us go."

I said, "No, Dad, let me handle this."

The state trooper came up to my window, and he was furious. He screamed, called me a few names, and told me I should lose my license, have my car impounded, and go to jail.

I apologized and waited for the decision.

He ended up writing me a $250 ticket and warned me to slow down. Dad was incredulous that I did not mention the suicides.

We finally got to Moab, and I worked with the school administration, staff, and students. That night we had a parent meeting, and my dad and I were asked to spend the night so we could attend a meeting with the community agencies the next day.

The following morning, I spent two to three hours with the community sharing our model in Provo. I reviewed the mistakes we had made, the lessons we had learned, and how critical it was to work together. School workers, police officers, firefighters, mental health workers, private providers, city leaders, and even the county attorney were there.

Toward the end of the afternoon, as we were wrapping up, someone asked how our trip down was and if we needed anything for the trip back. My father, who had been sitting in the back of the room reading a magazine, jumped up and said, "Yes, we do." I looked at him a little surprised, wondering what he meant.

He then pulled the ticket out of his coat pocket and said, "My son received a speeding ticket getting here. He was driving fine until the principal called and told him about the second suicide attempt." He then waved the ticket at the room.

My father went into detail on everything I had done wrong, how fast I was going, and how upset the officer was. I just sat and bowed my head. My father can get pretty emotional pretty fast.

I was a little embarrassed until the county attorney asked, "What county?" My father handed him the ticket, and he looked at it and said, "I'll take care of it." My father looked at me, smiled, and went back and sat down! It was the first and only speeding ticket I had ever had someone take care of. It also made my father's day!

Unfortunately, their community had three or four other suicides in a short period of time. Hearing about so many suicides so close to home was traumatizing for the youth as well as the adults. Most of the suicides were related to one another. A contagion like this, though rare, is a scary thing to have happen and to deal with. In my more than twenty years of experience, I would deal with three separate contagions. My heart went out to this community, but I was glad that I could help and spread the knowledge that we had learned in Provo.

⊙ LIFESAVER ⊙
TRAUMA

Trauma is defined as "an emotional response to a terrible event like an accident, rape or natural disaster"[1] or to other disturbing or distressing experiences. These experiences can "[recondition] the nervous system and can make the person maladaptive to a life of feeling safe and secure. The person experiencing the effects of trauma often does not have a normal baseline for emotion. This means that anger turns instantly to rage, and fear becomes instant terror. Another major symptom of trauma is the invasion of the past into the present. The traumatized person often relives the events and the associated emotions during waking, as pervasive fears and dread, and as nighttime terrors."[2]

These issues can take many years to subside, and it can take a long time for the traumatized person to feel in control again. Unfortunately, it seems that the issues from trauma can lead to other serious issues. Studies have found that trauma's effects could be linked to suicide.[3]

In addition to the effects listed above, effects of trauma could include many of the risk factors of suicide—depression, impulsiveness, isolation, anxiety, hopelessness, and despair—which account for the amount of trauma victims who do attempt or die by suicide.[4] Trauma in children has been found to be especially influential in the risk for suicide. This trauma includes sexual abuse, physical abuse, and parental domestic violence.

CALL TO ACTION

If you or anyone you know has had a traumatic experience, try taking the following steps[5]:

- ⟡ Acknowledge that the experience you had, whatever it was, was traumatic, but realize that the experience is over.
- ⟡ Instead of making major decisions while dealing with the aftereffects of a traumatic situation, make small decisions each day. This will help give you a sense of control.
- ⟡ Take care of yourself by exercising, eating well, and limiting your intake of caffeine.
- ⟡ When you're ready, talk about what happened or about what you are feeling with friends, family, a professional therapist, or a support group.

Losing someone to suicide or being involved at all in a suicide (attempting, responding, witnessing, etc.) is a traumatic experience. If you or your child has experienced this kind of trauma, contact your local mental health agency to be seen by a professional mental health expert.

NOTES

1. "Trauma," American Psychological Association, accessed March 7, 2018, http://www.apa.org/topics/trauma.
2. Jane Simington, "Childhood Trauma and Suicide," *Taking Flight International*, accessed March 8, 2018, http://takingflightinternational.com/suicide-intervention/who-suicide-intervention-is-for/relationship-between-childhood-trauma-and-suicide/.
3. Karen Dineen Wagner, "Effects of Childhood Trauma on Depression and Suicidality in Adulthood," *Psychiatric Times* 33, no. 11 (November 29, 2016), http://www.psychiatrictimes.com/child-adolescent-psychiatry/effects-childhood-trauma-depression-and-suicidality-adulthood.
4. "Facts about Trauma and Suicide," MCES, accessed March 7, 2018, http://www.mces.org/pages/suicide_fact_trauma.php.
5. Bulleted list summarizes information found at "Understanding Suicide and Grief: Experiencing Trauma," Support After Suicide, accessed March 3, 2018, http://www.supportaftersuicide.org.au/understanding-suicide-and-grief/experiencing-trauma.

CHAPTER 20

Committed to Helping Kids

Our year two in Provo City School District, though successful in not having any suicides, came with challenges. While I could not spend a lot of time on suicide prevention with all of my district assignments, I tried to spend as much time as I could visiting the schools, checking in with the administrators, and supporting the parents. Our community task force continued to meet monthly to review concerns and work on our goals.

We also continued to spend evenings and weekends training everyone we could. If you were an adult, we wanted to train you in suicide prevention. We were supported by our city leaders and numerous faith-based groups. If you were a youth, the Hope Squad training was teaching about suicide prevention. The Hope Squad kids continued to amaze us with their courage to reach out to help others.

One challenge in our second year was the number of threats and attempts. We continued to see many young people who wanted to hurt themselves. We had seventy attempts throughout the district. We hospitalized seven young people who were hurting and wanting to die.

One that stands out was a fifteen-year-old who had attempted three times before and was hospitalized twice. Her mother was at her wits' end trying to help her daughter and was doing all that she could. This young lady was dealing with severe mental health issues. Nedra, the local person in charge of the NAMI chapter for our area, reached out and got involved. It was so helpful for this family.

As mentioned earlier, NAMI is a great community resource run by volunteers. We have partnered with them since the beginning. Nedra asked me to come and do a presentation to a group of parents struggling with children who had severe mental illnesses. Although I was the teacher, in that meeting I became the student as they helped me understand their challenges and struggles.

I was touched by their love and commitment for their children. One mother shared a story about her son and how their family had used up all their resources to help him survive. She told me how many nights they stayed up to try and help him when he refused to stay on his medication. I admired their unconditional love for their family member. My heart goes out to the many families dealing with such overwhelming challenges. Seeing these families struggle also made me realize how important the resources were in our community and the need for these families to get help.

Another important person who helped us through challenges during year two was Miriam, who was a district social worker. She had been with the Department of Family Services before we recruited her. She was fantastic with the kids she worked with. Miriam is still one of the advisors for the Hope Squad. She loves interacting with the kids and frequently shares success stories with me.

Despite challenges that year, the positive feedback of Hope Squads continued. It is always refreshing when you receive positive feedback. Here is an email received from a parent:

> As a father, I want to personally thank you for the amazing job that the Hope Squad students are doing. Our daughter was struggling with depression, and we were not aware of it. She had confided in a friend, who also happened to be a Hope Squad member. The Hope Squad member convinced my daughter to talk to the school counselor. I was called and we were able to get her help.
>
> I hope all schools can have a Hope Squad. It is so important for young people to have someone to turn to when they are struggling. I had never even heard of the program before my daughter was helped. Thank you, Provo High!

Our community model was continuing to work in our city of one hundred thousand people. We had now trained more than ten thousand people from church to agencies to schools to neighbors. I was proud of the work that so many were involved in for our community.

Our yearly statewide suicide prevention conference was also starting to take off. As a community task force, we had partnered with Brigham Young University and Professor Melissa Heath to put on our first conference. That first conference had about 150 in attendance, and it had grown to include folks from all over the state. We were finally getting recognized as an organization committed to suicide prevention, intervention, and postvention. It also did not hurt that we were bringing in experts from all over to help educate everyone on the latest research in prevention.

CONTINUING WITH
ZERO SUICIDES

We were on to year three with no suicides. As a district, we could not believe it. Some of the "naysayers" said it had nothing to do with what we were doing even though we were the ones identifying kids struggling and getting parents involved.

At the end of year three, I had a principal remark to me, "So, three years without a suicide. I assume that we will stop all of this suicide prevention training we have been doing for the past three years."

I smiled and said, "Actually, the result of no suicides is the main reason we will keep training."

We hospitalized five kids that year as a direct result of a referral from one of the Hope Squad students or trained staff members. I cannot say enough about the community and its commitment to helping us prevent suicides. It takes a passionate person to help keep everyone organized and committed. I was lucky because I had a dozen amazing, committed leaders who wanted to do all they could to save lives.

I also appreciated knowing that these agencies "had my back." I was always being challenged by someone who believed the Hope Squads would never work and that it was a bad idea. However, when someone who doubted had a chance to meet with the Hope Squad advisors and their members, in every case the person walked away impressed and having a changed opinion.

One such advisor was Chris, an outstanding Hope Squad advisor at Independence High School. His Hope Squad had some of the toughest kids in the district. When we would meet with all the advisors, he would share inspiring stories and examples of what his kids were doing to save lives. We were learning that the Hope Squad could be successful in any setting if you had the right support from administration and a passionate advisor.

Time was flying by with the success of the Hope Squad. In the past, when we would have a suicide, time seemed to go by slowly. Sometimes it would take months to recover. We were finding that with the Hope Squad, it took two to three years to change the culture of a school. It's not easy convincing the rest of the students that it is okay to get help when you are struggling.

I could feel and see it when I visited the schools. Some of the teachers who were naysayers in the past were starting to come around. They would even reach out to me to share an experience they had with one of the Hope Squad kids. It was exciting to see the changes in the school culture.

Though it was taking time to change the schools (and, unfortunately, some school administrators and counselors who had not caught the vision yet),

Hope Squads were already changing the community. Hope Squads seek to reduce self-destructive behavior and youth suicide by training, building, and creating change, and they were doing a wonderful job.

SEEING THE REWARDS
OF OUR EFFORTS

It was 2008, year four with the Hope Squads, and still no suicides. To be honest, no one was expecting another year without a suicide. We thought it was impossible to keep seeing such success year after year, and those who doubted the program kept reminding me that "it was just a matter of time" before we lost another child. While I knew they were right, I still had a lot of faith in the young people who were working so hard to prevent another one.

I was constantly reminded that not all suicides can be prevented, and it's true. Too many young people are dealing with serious mental illness issues. Add trauma from earlier childhood issues, and it can be deadly for these kids. We knew the challenges were real, but we still tried to do all that we could.

During year four, we had twenty-four attempts and hospitalized only two children. When we reviewed the year as a task force, we realized that all the work everyone was doing was paying off. More families were being trained on how to recognize warning signs and asking for help instead of ignoring or hoping it would go away.

Even our emergency room folks were sharing that they were starting to see a stabilizing effect across our community. The communities around us were growing and dealing with more attempts and suicides than we were. In fact, most people outside of Provo did not believe us. One person at our conference said to me, "Four years in Provo without a youth suicide. I don't believe it."

But I was grateful for people who did believe it and I believed in the Hope Squads. One such person was Bob Gentry, the director of personnel for the school district. He was one of my best friends and mentors. He had been a middle school principal when I was at the high school. At the district office, we spent a lot of time together working on challenges and problems across the district.

We were out for lunch one time and he said to me, "I know that many folks in Provo will remember you as a great high school principal for the things you did to help struggling families succeed; however, what most people will probably never know is the work that you have done behind the scenes to save so many lives. Your skill set is the ability to bring people together for a cause and then empower them to achieve it."

That was one of the nicest things anyone has ever said to me. While I wish I could take the credit for the success, it would not be fair to the many who have worked so hard behind the scenes.

A perfect example was a communications professor named Jay Fox from Brigham Young University. We had met through training and I knew we needed him on our task force. He joined us and spent the next year putting together training for the media and press on how to report suicides. It was priceless and helped us as a community reduce sensationalism with suicide.

Heather was another example. She was our lead social worker for the school district. She was bright, dedicated, and passionate about suicide prevention. She was one of the stars that made sure the Hope Squads were successful. She had been another one that we had recruited from a state agency. She loved kids and you could tell.

Another "behind the scenes" person was Ron Vigoren, a local business owner who loved helping the school district with projects. He and I were members of the local Rotary Club and he did all he could to help us succeed. He was the calming voice of reason to our school board.

I loved seeing so many people working together for suicide prevention. I also loved hearing how the program was helping people. One time I was invited to do a training session at a middle school, and the counselor asked me to come and present on my standard "Suicide 101" presentation. The principal and counselor had warned me that the parents did not want to talk about suicide and were against having a Hope Squad in their school.

By now I have given this presentation hundreds of times, so I was getting comfortable in front of people. But halfway through my presentation, I could tell I was in trouble. Not one person was looking at me with interest or in agreement. As I stumbled through it and finished, I knew they were not going to change their minds. Then one of the mothers raised her hand and asked to share her story. When she was done, there was not a dry eye anywhere and everyone had changed their mind about having a Hope Squad. She shared this email with me the day after the presentation.

Dr. Hudnall,

I was the woman who commented on the Hope Squad program this last Monday. I hope you didn't mind me making those comments; it isn't something I usually do, but I felt very compelled to do so. The parents need to know what an amazing program this is and how much it not only benefits those students who are in emotional need but also those students, like my son, who love helping others and genuinely care about their welfare. We knew he loved being on Hope Squad. We talked a lot about it, yet sadly it wasn't until he lost his own life in a car crash that we truly understood how his reaching out and being kind to others was such a blessing in their lives.

My son was a capella president, wrestling champion, and an all-around good person. I feel that Hope Squad is a life raft in the school system. I am so grateful for all you have done and continue to do for those students who need help and are calling out. Hearing why you started the program and seeing all that has been accomplished since it began helped me to understand the true need that exists for us to be involved and have our eyes and ears open.

Our youngest daughter was nominated to be in the middle school's Hope Squad. She is honored and can't wait to be a part of something that meant so much to her brother. She is so much like him and has a caring, compassionate heart.

Thank you for such a wonderful program!

Another time, my wife, MiLinda, and I were at my favorite ice-cream store when a gentleman walked up to me and said, "You're the suicide guy, aren't you?" I smiled as I waited for my ice cream and replied that I was. He smiled and said, "I want to thank you for the Hope Squad! My daughter was a member for four years, and it was the best thing ever. She loved being on it. Once a month she would come home and make our family sit down so she could train and practice what she had learned on her family."

I thanked him, and then he said, "What I really want to share is that she has been gone for three years out of state to college. About two weeks ago, my wife and I were in the kitchen when we heard our teenage son talking to a friend on his cell phone. The more we listened, the more we realized that he had a friend who was struggling, and our son was helping him.

"The amazing thing was that he was using all the things his sister had taught him from her time on the Hope Squad. Thank you for such a wonderful program. It has benefited our family!"

He made my day!

It was rewarding to see that the community efforts and the efforts of the Hope Squad members were making such a positive difference in people's lives.

Those efforts carried into year five with Hope Squads, and there was still not one suicide! Our numbers for referrals and hospitalization continued to decrease with twenty-three referrals for help and only five young people hospitalized during that year. Even the CEO of the hospital made a comment to me about it: "Keep this up, Greg, and you may put the psych unit out of business, which is the best thing that could happen in our community!"

I loved seeing and hearing about our success.

OUTLINING OBJECTIVES
FOR HOPE SQUADS

The first objective of the Hope Squad membership is to be trained in recognizing suicide warning signs and, most important, to act upon those signs. The key is to identify peers with undetected, untreated, or emerging mental illnesses. About 50 percent of mental illness cases begin by age fourteen,[1] which makes it critical for the Hope Squad students to realize when a fellow student may be experiencing a mental illness.

The second objective is to build positive relationships among peers and faculty in schools to facilitate acceptance for students seeking help.

A story comes to mind that goes along with this objective. One day, I got a call from Kay, a middle school principal, and she shared the following story.

"I had an amazing young lady at my school. While she was very successful, she struggled with depression and anxiety. During the middle of the year, her family moved to California. Unfortunately, while there, the young lady took her life by suicide.

"About a month after the suicide, the mother picked up her daughter's belongings from the police department. When she got home, she plugged her daughter's phone in to charge it. When she looked at it later, the last text her daughter had sent was to her friends in Utah at her old school. The message said, 'I wish my school had a Hope Squad here. You were so kind and supportive when I was struggling there.'"

The mother had called Kay to say she wanted a Hope Squad in every school in California. Though this was sad news, I felt inspired that Hope Squads were making a difference!

The last objective for the Hope Squad program is to change the school culture regarding suicide by reducing the stigmas about mental illness. It takes time and can often be very challenging.

✪ LIFESAVER ✪
GETTING HELP FOR MENTAL
ILLNESSES AND DEPRESSION

Like suicide, major mental illnesses rarely just happen one day. Those with the mental illness or those around them can often notice that something is changing before the mental illness develops completely.[2] This is why it is important for parents, peers (including Hope Squad members), teachers, and the individuals with the mental illness to be able to recognize those changes, especially at a young age, when the symptoms are usually first showing.

Here are some of the signs and symptoms[3] of mental illness:

○ Feelings of extreme fear or nervousness, as well as feeling disconnected
○ Lack of interest to engage in activities and withdrawal from any social settings
○ An unusual decrease in performance or functioning in school, social setting, or other settings
○ Dramatic or fast change in emotions
○ Change in appearance or hygiene habits
○ Extreme changes in appetite or sleep
○ Odd or unusual behavior
○ Illogical thinking or problems thinking or concentrating
○ An avoidance of situations that overstimulate the senses or having a higher sensitivity to senses

Here are additional signs and symptoms[4] that apply specifically to depression, a mental illness common in those who attempt or are lost to suicide:

○ Unexpected weight loss or gain and changes in appetite
○ Insomnia or sleeping too much
○ Feelings of deep sadness or worthlessness
○ Thoughts of wanting to die
○ Poor concentration or decision-making
○ Lack of energy for or interest in once-loved activities

These symptoms must last a minimum of two weeks before it can be diagnosed as depression.[5]

Although these are common signs and symptoms of mental illness and depression, having or seeing just one or two doesn't necessarily mean someone has a mental illness. The symptoms could be from other medical conditions or result from grief or other losses in life. But if someone has three or four or more occurring at once and they are interfering with that person's day-to-day functioning, it may be worthwhile to visit a mental health professional.[6]

CALL TO ACTION

Learn how to recognize the early warning signs of mental illness. If you feel concerned that your child may have a mental illness, take him or her to be evaluated by a mental health professional. The earlier you get help, the more of a chance you have to delay or minimize the symptoms.[7]

It's also important to recognize warning signs and symptoms of depression early on so that the depression does not worsen or lead to negative situations.

Thankfully, there are many treatments for depression. In fact, depression is one of the most treatable mental disorders.[8] If someone you know is depressed, take them to be evaluated by a mental health professional. They will have suggestions for medication, therapies, or self-help strategies.

NOTES

1. "Warning Signs of Mental Illness," American Psychiatric Association, accessed March 26, 2018, https://www.psychiatry.org/patients-families/warning-signs-of-mental-illness.
2. Ibid.
3. Adapted from information found at "Warning Signs of Mental Illness," American Psychiatric Association.
4. Adapted from information found at "What Is Depression?" American Psychiatric Association, accessed March 26, 2018, https://www.psychiatry.org/patients-families /depression/what-is-depression.
5. Ibid.
6. "Warning Signs of Mental Illness," American Psychiatric Association.
7. Ibid.
8. "What Is Depression?" American Psychiatric Association.

CHAPTER 21

Never Stop Working to Save Lives

Despite all the success we were having and the good things that came from the Hope Squad, year six was another challenging year. We had thirty-nine young people threaten or attempt, and we hospitalized nine—our numbers had gone up from the previous year. It was hard to see an increase in those numbers after they had been slowly decreasing.

One of the things we worked on that year was to recognize the difference between the low-risk and the high-risk suicidal student. Dr. Melissa Heath, a professor at Brigham Young University, helped us understand the difference and the importance of intervening when dealing with a high-risk student.

In the past, we treated all the kids the same when we found out they were suicidal, but we were realizing we needed to do more to separate the two. Our lead district social worker, Heather, helped us formulate a way to define the two types of risk.

Low risk was applied to students who talked about hurting themselves or about wanting to die but did not have a plan or access to a weapon. While we still treated the situation seriously and always involved parents, we did not take them to the hospital. If the parent asked for additional help, we would refer them to Wasatch Mental Health.

High risk was applied to the students who made comments about wanting to die, who sometimes gave a personal item of value to a friend, or who even made a plan and had access to a weapon. In these situations, we would always involve our school resource officer and would do all that we could to get them to the emergency room. The parents were grateful for the intervention, and I was appreciative of the support from everyone.

The biggest challenge during year six was inside the system, not outside. Once again, I had administrators asking why we had to keep focusing so much on suicide prevention, because there hadn't been a suicide in six years. The issue came up when we scheduled training for our bus drivers and lunch workers.

Some of the principals complained to the district director that it was too much time off and that they had many more compelling things to cover.

The director even mentioned it in our cabinet meeting, and I had to bite my tongue and hold my breath (quiet dignity) so I would not scream. The superintendent could see my frustration and jumped in to help. I was proud of his remarks: "Actually, I think the suicide prevention training is important and something we need to support regardless of what others may think." I was grateful he was supportive and taking the lead on such an important topic.

Addressing Concerns about Being on the Hope Squad

One day, I was invited to a parent meeting for Hope Squad members. The students put on the training for their parents, and I was impressed with the results. The students conducted the meeting, reviewed the curriculum with their parents, and then answered questions. Even the parents were impressed.

After the meeting, one of the moms came up to me and said, "Dr. Hudnall, I have some concerns about my son being on the Hope Squad."

When I asked her what the concerns were, she replied, "My son is always looking for friends who are struggling. He will stay up at night checking on friends, and he will skip classes to seek out someone who is struggling. I worry about him being on the Hope Squad."

I listened and then asked, "What was he like before he was on the Hope Squad?"

She replied, "He was always looking for friends who are struggling. He would stay up at night checking on friends, and he would skip classes to seek out someone who was struggling."

I laughed and replied, "Don't you think that is probably the reason he was referred by his peers? He is always watching out for them, regardless of being on the Hope Squad. Why don't you give him a year with our program, and let's see if we can help him balance his life."

About six months later, I ran into this mother at a school event. She came up to me and reported that whatever we were doing was right on. Her son was learning appropriate boundaries and was starting to take care of himself while still taking care of others. She thanked me for the program.

We continued to work on improving our program. Through our state-wide conference on suicide prevention, I had the chance to work with Dr. Phil Rogers, who was a researcher working with the American Foundation for Suicide Prevention (AFSP). He was bright, articulate, and passionate about suicide prevention. We invited him to be our keynote speaker for one of our conferences. In return, he became a dear friend and a mentor.

He spent a few days in Utah helping us with our Hope Squad curriculum and evaluating our research. He was supportive of how we had created our courses for fourth through sixth grade, seventh through eighth grade, and ninth through twelfth grade. He reviewed everything and gave great feedback. As per his feedback, we worked with the University of Utah and implemented a pre and post survey for every Hope Squad member to take.

With this survey, Dr. Rogers suggested that we add one question. He felt that many outsiders could think that being on the Hope Squad would create too much pressure for the students. He said, "Let's ask the kids and see what they say."

So we did. We added one question to the survey: "Is being on the Hope Squad too much pressure for you?" I am excited to share that the University of Utah has done four years of research with thousands of Hope Squad members. In response to this question, 84 percent of those young people responded that it is not too much pressure. In fact, most kids will say that they need this type of education because the kids are coming to them anyway.

Outside of the research, an experience that showed Hope Squad was a good kind of pressure happened at one of our Hope Squad conferences for all members of Hope Squad. The conference is held every March by the community crisis team. Our state Hope Squad student officers, who are nominated by their advisors, help put it on. These are some of the most talented kids I have ever worked with.

KSL television reported on this conference.[1] During an interview, one of the reporters asked one of the Hope Squad presidents, "Do you think being on the Hope Squad is too much pressure?"

The student's response was right on when she replied,

> You old folks think we never discuss it. The reality is that we talk about it all the time. When I was in the seventh grade, my best friend was going to kill himself. I stayed up for two weeks every night trying to convince him not to do it. I was finally able to get my dad's help. He was able to talk to my friend's parents and they got him help.
>
> Two years later, I was nominated to the Hope Squad. I was gone when they explained what it was in the classrooms. When I was back at school, the counselor called me down and told me I was nominated by my peers to a program called the Hope Squad. I asked, "What the heck is a Hope Squad?" When she explained it to me, I literally had tears in my eyes.
>
> This is exactly what I have been looking for. If only I had known then what I know now, I might have been able to intervene earlier with my friend when I would have recognized the signs.

I love being a Hope Squad member. I love helping others and knowing what to do when a friend is struggling. I also love the way it changed my school. My fellow students actually feel like there is someone out there that they can talk to when they are struggling.

This student and many more like her have been making positive changes in her school. Thank goodness for Hope Squad members who recognize those who are struggling and have the courage to intervene. Those members were the ones who made having a school year with no suicides a reality.

CONTINUING TO MOVE FORWARD DESPITE CHANGE AND CHALLENGES

At that time, I had been teaching in the evening as an adjunct professor at Brigham Young University. My class was about social work in the school setting, and of course I included information about suicide prevention. It was fun for me to be with such talented young people.

One day, the dean of the department asked me to stop by his office to meet with him after one of my classes. When I stopped by, we talked about a few academic issues, and then he said, "I want you to know that you have been nominated as the Adjunct Professor of the Year." I was stunned. While I knew I worked hard to have fun, interesting classes, I did not think I was that great of a professor.

When I shared this with the dean, he laughed. He then said, "While your nomination was based on great teaching and positive feedback from your students, the real reason is the difference you are making in our community with suicide prevention. You have dedicated your life to saving lives through education. You even teach your students suicide prevention here at BYU. While that is not even in the curriculum, you know it's important."

Once again, word was getting out that suicide prevention is critical to the success of saving lives. It cannot be one or even a few passionate people carrying it forward. It takes the commitment of the entire community. I was grateful for the recognition and the tender mercy shown by my academic colleagues.

Beside being an adjunct professor, I was now also the associate superintendent for the school district. Things were changing in our community. Many of our original task force members were moving on—either retiring or getting new assignments. Dr. Ken Tuttle retired as the director of psychiatric care for the hospital, and Mark Payne retired as the superintendent of the hospital. Reverend Jackson moved, and we missed his spiritual leadership. I could feel it in the air: Board members and others were looking for more change.

With all this change, I realized that we were losing citywide support for the focus on suicide prevention. It was not on purpose; it was more of the loss of kindred spirits who had been in the trenches from the beginning. Our hours of commitment had helped us bond together. When you experience a suicide and spend hours responding, a kind of a bonding takes place, sort of like soldiers in a foxhole. You may make a mistake, but everyone on your team knows your intention and passion. The support for one another was strong; however, with people moving on, I could tell that things were going to be different.

One of the first calls for help I received after all that change was from a school district up north. On Sunday, the student body vice president had taken her life, and on Monday, the student body vice president at another school in the district took his life.

Instead of responding to the crisis with Dr. Tuttle, who had retired, I went with Dan Daley, who had replaced him. We were asked to provide help and training for the parent meeting being held that Tuesday night.

Because the school district was a few hours away, Dan and I had a chance to visit on the trip. He had been on our crisis team for years and was a stable member when we needed help. Along with me and Doran Williams from Wasatch Mental Health, he now was a coleader for the Utah County Hope Task Force.

Dan shared with me the increase he was seeing in referrals for kids needing help. He talked about how it was happening countrywide, not just in Provo. He told me to "hang on" and predicted it would be a challenging year.

Dan was right. Year eight was the year we were in trouble. The very first week of school, we had an attempt that could have been a suicide. It was the help of peers that once again helped us through a difficult situation.

With over fifty-two attempts and ten young people hospitalized, year eight turned out to be our toughest year yet, with the highest number of hospitalizations and threats and attempts we'd ever had. I was worried that we had probably become a little lax with so much success.

One positive aspect of year eight was how much the Hope Squads were changing the culture in schools. One principal shared with me that he had been an administrator for many years, but it wasn't until he had a Hope Squad that he started to see the "cultural change" in his school; people were actually talking about mental illness!

He shared that parents would come into his office and shut the door and tell him, "I am worried about my son's teammate," or someone would come in and say, "I am worried about my daughter's boyfriend." When he would ask why, they would share a behavior they had seen or a comment they had heard.

He told me, "I believe the Hope Squad was the program that was helping change that culture. Now even kids that are not members of the Hope

Squad are letting counselors know they have friends they are worried about. It was almost as if the Hope Squad gave us permission to talk about mental health issues."

This positive comment was both wonderful and needed during a difficult year. I was worried about the impact of these challenges on our schools. The hospitalization of ten students was a particularly big issue. It meant that at least once a month we were identifying a young person who was intent on hurting themselves.

On one difficult case, I was at the emergency room after a student was placed in the hospital. I was shaken up, and the emergency room social worker, who happened to be a former student of mine, came over to visit with me.

We visited for a while and then he asked how I was doing. I replied that it had been a tough night. He then looked at me and said, "I know this can be very emotionally draining for you. I also know that you think you have to save the world of young people from suicide. While I admire that, please always remember that you cannot save everyone. Some kids have made up their mind to do everything they can to leave this world."

When he left, I realized he was right. Though I was counting our blessings for the past eight years without a suicide, I knew that it was just a matter of time before we lost a student. However, I also realized that I would not give up. We may lose a child to suicide, but if we do, it will not be because we have not tried to do everything we can to save just one more.

FIGHTING TO MAINTAIN SUCCESS

At the beginning of our ninth year of having Hope Squads in our school district, there was once again a change at the top. Superintendent Merrill retired, and a new superintendent came to Provo from Washington State. Our school board was changing, and new challenges were on the horizon.

One of the challenges was keeping the number of suicides at zero. Year nine reminded me of my favorite holiday movie, *It's a Wonderful Life*. Remember the scene when everybody makes a run on George Bailey and Uncle Billy's bank and loan company? George convinced them to hold tight and started handing out money to hold people over until things settled down. When everyone was gone, George and Uncle Billy held the last two dollars in their hands as they counted down the clock to another day. They had survived, but only just.

During year nine, we felt like we were scrambling and fighting to keep suicide out of our schools. On the last day of school, we held our breath. We had had way too many suicide attempts and referrals, with 110 kids attempting and thirteen kids hospitalized, but not one student was lost to suicide the entire school year. I felt like shouting for joy.

The day after our last graduation, my district colleagues and I were in my office talking about the school year. One of the staff members mentioned that this was our ninth year without a suicide! I wanted to cry. I can honestly tell you that we did not talk about the years of success even though we did talk about the data. We got so caught up in training and educating and responding to attempts and suicides out of our district that we sometimes forgot to celebrate the successes. Going nine years without a suicide was a big deal, especially for our Provo district, which had been struggling so much.

Working Hard Together

Once again, we heard the comment that it was a miracle. But we knew better. It was hard work from a lot of people who were committed to saving lives. What most people did not see was all the training and support that was happening in our community. At one point, I counted over five hundred volunteers and workers throughout the city. This included those involved in our school training, our annual walk, the Hope Squads, the community crisis team, and numerous health fairs.

Over the past fifteen years, the community task force had trained more than twenty-five thousand kids, teachers, parents, and community members in suicide prevention. Over the past nine years of the Hope Squads being implemented, we had hospitalized ninety-one students in partnership with our local mental health agency, law enforcement, and hospital. Another hundred kids were hospitalized on their own by their parents. Many of these parents had been trained and knew what to look for. It was a community-wide effort.

We have had hundreds of Hope Squad members making a difference in the lives of their peers. Over the years, I would run into a former Hope Squad student who was then in college or married. They would share the difference the Hope Squad had made in their life and how they had made a difference in the lives of their peers. One graduate student shared that she used the training from her Hope Squad to help her with roommates and a spouse.

Dr. George Bayless, the principal of Timpview High School, shared that he loved having the Hope Squad on his campus. He related how difficult it was to deal with so many attempts and suicides before the Hope Squad was started. He said, "I know that there were numerous instances where a Hope Squad student was responsible for the prevention of suicide attempts. The Hope Squad brought an awareness to our entire student body of the need for everyone to be actively engaged in suicide prevention. Without a doubt, the Hope Squad's efforts saved lives."

Were lives saved? YES! Was it hard work? Again, YES! Harder than anything I have ever experienced emotionally, physically, and, at times, spiritually.

Despite our success, the years were not picture-perfect. During those fifteen years, we had more than nine hundred threats and more than that in attempts. I am sure there were hundreds more that we were not even aware of and even hundreds more that parents were not aware of. Many of those who attempted could have been a suicide if it were not for a concerned family member or friend who reached out in time.

As we worked together as members of the community, mental health professionals, and students, our mantra really did work—"While it takes an entire village to raise a child, we know it takes an entire community to save one."

It had been (and still is) a long trip on the road to suicide prevention, but to me, it has been well worth the journey.

❍ LIFESAVER ❍
PERMISSION GRANTED

In the past, I used to get calls for help or advice from my educational colleagues in Utah. Now I receive them from law enforcement, city leaders, clergy members, and moms and dads in distress. These folks on the other end of the phone are well educated, bright, caring, and, in most cases, afraid. They are afraid because they cannot "fix" their child's problem or make their pain go away. We as loving parents hurt when our child hurts. We also remember the experiences from our lives, especially painful ones from childhood. We do not want our child to have to go through what we did.

But we forget that, in reality, many of those experiences made us stronger. Sure, they hurt at the time and may still hurt when we think about them. But trying to take away our child's pain may also take their opportunity to experience the pain and learn from it, to try to manage it.

Instead of eliminating pain, Dr. Jack Klott, one of my all-time-favorite suicidologists, suggests the following:

> The goal of suicide is the elimination of pain. This pain may be due to a mental illness, a tragic loss, a personal failure, a destitute life, loneliness. In many ways, our prevention efforts are also oriented towards "elimination of pain." However, we need a more realistic focus on "coping" with pain as opposed to "eliminating" pain. Teaching our children how to cope would be an excellent starting point to suicide prevention. Suicide, in its essence, is a result of a failure in the individual's capacity to cope.[2]

Like this remarkable author and therapist, I suggest that instead of "fixing" our children's pain and struggles, we should try to help them learn to deal with pain, as I discussed in the Coping and Problem-Solving Skills Lifesaver. That way, when your children come across painful situations (and they will; everyone does), they are prepared to handle that pain in a constructive way.

In many of my parent training sessions, I discuss this "inability to deal with the psychological failure"[3] that Dr. Klott discusses. Many parents will raise their hands and ask, "How do I do that when my child is suffering?" The answer is not simple, as Dr. Klott stated:

> We have, unfortunately, medicalized and biologized suicide. We often hear that depression causes suicide. That is a tragically misleading comment. There is no one isolated causal entity in regards to suicide. There is no golden key to explain this tragedy.
>
> We also know that suicide is the result of a complexity of issues. It is the sad result of varied stressors, causing individually defined agony, for which the person has no capacity to cope.
>
> Today's suicide prevention efforts are, more often than not, focused on the early detection and treatment of mood and anxiety disorders. Is this a worthwhile endeavor? It certainly is. Will this decrease the rate of suicide in our society? It helps . . . but it is not the total answer.[4]

My heart goes out to all those who are suffering from the effects of suicide ideation. Suicide is complicated, with no simple, catch-all solution, which is why we all need to work together to prevent further suffering caused by suicide.

In closing, I want to share a suggestion that I leave with my audiences when I am finishing a lecture or presentation. We as a society have moved away from parenting to wanting to be our kids' friends or being too busy to parent. I get it. Life can be hectic and even overwhelming, but with social media, cyberbullying, and everything else, we need to parent now more than ever.

My closing thought comes from something that I learned from one of our mental health advisors, Christine. She called it her "parent permission" session. Too many parents choose to be more like a friend than like a parent to their children. One time her young client in therapy shared that he wished his parents would act more like a parent and less like a friend. He said that although he may show on the outside that he resented their intrusion, on the inside he knew it was because they cared about him.

Christine also shared an interesting concept. She said that when she meets with a struggling young person, she always likes to meet with the parents. One of the things she tells them is, "It's okay to be a parent and to try your best. You're going to make mistakes, but please be the parent and do the parent things that your child needs."

So I am giving you permission to get angry, be frustrated, ask questions, share concerns, take away privileges, and even ground your child when necessary. I am giving you permission to make the tough call and to even have your kids get mad at you.

I am granting you permission to be a parent!

Through the years, I have found that the role of parenting has taken a back seat. While there are many reasons, many excuses, and many obstacles, I believe it is time to take back parenting.

Being a parent to your child is so important.

Call to Action

There are times when our child is suffering and under stress, and this will require us to respond and intervene differently than normal. When the behavior is out of the "normal behavior," we may need additional help to address it.

Below are general guidelines[5] you can use to support your children during times of stress.

- Listen.
- Don't avoid difficult conversations.
- Acknowledge that we don't have all the answers.
- Monitor the TV and internet.
- Be prepared.
- Be aware and sensitive to your children's responses.
- Take care of yourself.
- Spend time as a family.
- Encourage hope.
- Have at least one meal a day together.

I once read that "in times of adversity and turmoil, stress evokes strong emotions and causes uncertainty in all of us. As parents, we are in the best position to help our children."[6] Again, I am granting you permission to be a parent. Your child needs you, and being an involved parent is one of the first steps you can take toward preventing suicide.

Notes

1. The story can be found at https://www.ksl.com/?nid=148&sid=33910736.
2. Klott, "Suicide and Psychological Pain: Prevention That Works," 134.
3. Ibid.
4. Ibid.
5. Adapted from "Supporting Your Children in Times of Stress," AFNATAL: Israel Trauma and Resiliency Center, accessed January 19, 2018, https://www.afnatal.org/supporting-your-children-in-times-of-stress.
6. Ibid.

AFTERWORD

Update 2018

We never thought Hope Squads would extend beyond the Provo City School District. In 2013, I was invited to testify before the Utah legislature by Representative Steve Eliason. When I finished, Pamela Atkins, the governor's assistant, grabbed me and said, "We want Hope Squads in every school in Utah!"

Steve has been our biggest champion by sponsoring numerous bills for suicide prevention in Utah. The Hope Squads are now partially funded by the Utah legislature. We also continue to be supported by Intermountain Healthcare, the Savage Family Foundation, and others.

In July 2013, I decided to retire at age fifty-four as the associate superintendent. I am living my dream of doing suicide prevention full-time and working to take Hope Squads throughout the state of Utah and across the United States.

As of 2018, Hope Squads are in 284 schools (K–12) in Utah. Hope Squads are also in schools in Alaska, Washington, Wyoming, Texas, Idaho, Nebraska, Indiana, Arizona, Oklahoma, Minnesota, and Canada, and they are soon to be in Ohio and Wisconsin. We have more than ten thousand Hope Squad students who leave their house every single day with a desire to help a friend who may be struggling.

Through the Hope Squad program, thousands of kids have been referred by their peers to an adult for help. Hundreds have been hospitalized and many have received help with their mental health challenge while others were able to know that someone cared about them.

We are an evidence-based tier-3 program in the state of Utah, as approved by our state evidenced-based review board. This basically means that our program has consistently shown positive results in our method of intervention. We continue to look for funding through grants and donations to do research and be approved on the national evidenced-based register. We have partnered with the University of Cincinnati, the University of Utah, and Brigham Young University for ongoing research to continue improving our program.

I continue to work with and support Provo City School District with their crisis team and with training all employees in suicide prevention every three years. My replacement as assistant superintendent, Gary Wilson, has embraced the vision and is continuing the focus on prevention.

We have trained more than forty-five thousand people in suicide prevention, intervention, and postvention.

We are in sixty-five cities in Utah and have established statewide partnerships with the mental health agencies and twenty-four Intermountain Healthcare hospitals.

We have continued with our statewide suicide prevention conference. We now invite all the western states. We have some of the best and brightest presenters from across the country. If you would like to attend, please visit our website (hopesquad.com) to learn more.

If your community is looking to come together to prevent suicides or if your school is interested in having a Hope Squad, feel free to contact us. Our contact information is on our website, hopesquad.com. Please remember that you cannot have a Hope Squad without a partnership with your local mental health agency.

I am proud to let you know that Timpview High School has not had a suicide in fourteen years. We know that we cannot prevent every suicide, but we will continue to do all we can to prevent one.

Finally, thank you for reading my book. I would love to hear your thoughts. My email address is greg@hopesquad.com.

ABOUT THE AUTHOR

Dr. Gregory A. Hudnall is a former high school principal, student service director, and associate superintendent with the Provo City School District. He has been involved with suicide prevention for the past twenty years. He is the founder of HOPE4UTAH, a nonprofit grassroots community organization dedicated to suicide prevention, intervention, and postvention in Utah. The school-based program "HOPE Squads" has been responsible for over 2,500 students referred for help and is in over 300 schools.

Scan to visit

hope4utah.com